Project Reviews, Assurance and Governance

For Caroline

Project Reviews, Assurance and Governance

GRAHAM OAKES

Routledge
Taylor & Francis Group

LONDON AND NEW YORK

First published in paperback 2024

First published 2008 by Gower Publishing

Published 2016 by Routledge
4 Park Square, Milton Park, Abingdon, Oxon OX14 4RN

and by Routledge
605 Third Avenue, New York, NY 10158

Routledge is an imprint of the Taylor & Francis Group, an informa business

British Library Cataloguing in Publication Data
Oakes, Graham
 Project reviews, assurance and governance
 1. Project management 2. Project management - Case studies
 I. Title
 658.4'04

Library of Congress Cataloging-in-Publication Data
Oakes, Graham.
 Project reviews, assurance, and governance / by Graham Oakes.
   p. cm.
 Includes bibliographical references and index.
 ISBN 978-0-566-08807-0
 1. Project management. 2. Project management--Case studies. I. Title.

 HD69.P75O24 2008
 658.4'04--dc22

                                                                                    2008015661

ISBN 13: 978-0-566-08807-0 (hbk)
ISBN 13: 978-1-03-283803-8 (pbk)
ISBN 13: 978-1-315-60246-2 (ebk)

DOI: 10.4324/9781315602462

Contents

List of Figures

List of Tables

Acknowledgements

Many people helped with this book. I've learned from project teams as we bounced ideas around in the course of reviews. I've learned from review teams as we puzzled together about how to conduct reviews, or about how to get people to listen to our findings. The people who participated in my training course *Conducting Effective Project Reviews* taught me a lot. Project sponsors and executives taught me many things as we worked together to steer projects and portfolios. That makes a cast of thousands. I'd like to thank them all.

I'd particularly like to thank the people who helped with case studies, and who reviewed the manuscript for the book – Bent Adsersen, Laurent Bossavit, Nynke Fokma, Payson Hall, Sarah Kittmer, Judith Lane, Lynn Lyon, Phil Stubbington. And especial thanks to my wife, Caroline Hawkridge, for her help, support, critical comments and love over the years.

Of course, any mistakes, gaps or omissions in the book, I made all by myself.

PART I

Introduction

CASE STUDY

Earthquakes in the Project Portfolio

Computer games are a serious business. A game for a current generation console (say an Xbox® or Playstation® 3) can cost $20 million or more to build. Even back in the mid-1990s, when my experience with formal project reviews began, a game could easily cost $2 million to develop. The company I worked for had about 60 such games under development at any one time.

My company, like most in the industry, had a problem. Projects slipped. They often slipped by months or even years. This didn't do a lot to help our reputation with retailers, reviewers and customers. Perhaps even more critically for people who cared about things like making payroll, it made it impossible to predict cashflow. I was part of a team that was set up to bring predictability to project delivery.

Each member of the team was responsible for providing an independent view of the status of about ten projects in the portfolio. Each week we looked at what our projects were producing and tracked this against the original milestone schedules. We tracked the status of key risks. We read status reports. Above all, we talked with the project managers, discussing the issues they were dealing with and listening to their concerns. Sometimes we offered suggestions or put them in touch with other people who were dealing with similar issues, but often we just functioned as a sounding board to help them think through what was going on.

We also produced a weekly report for senior management – the Director of Development and the Chief Financial Officer (CFO). This consisted of a simple ordered listing of the projects under development, ranked by our assessment of their level of risk. We also wrote one or two sentences on each project, summarizing our reasons for its ranking. This report was openly published to everyone in the company, which gave everyone plenty of chance to tell us where we'd got it wrong…

(Interestingly, project managers generally reckoned their project was riskier than we'd assessed it. The project managers' line management generally thought projects were less risky than we'd assessed them. Either way, people started to actively track the positioning of their project, and to tell us how our ranking of its status could be improved. By publishing our report openly, we created a very useful channel for this information.)

After we'd been working with our projects for a while, we began to recognize a pattern. Projects would go through a couple of fairly formal investment-approval reviews when they were set up. They'd then run quietly for six or 12 months. Then, about three months before the date they were due to be delivered into testing, they'd start to slip. Often they'd have a big slip initially, followed by a series of progressively smaller slips as they got closer to the end date (see Figure S1.1).

This pattern was remarkably consistent. Because we were working with a portfolio of 60 similar projects, we could draw graphs and start to see statistical trends. We found a strong correlation between the magnitude of each slip and the length of time left until the due date for delivery into testing (see Figure S1.2). For some reason, projects would remain stable for much of their development phase, then suddenly experience a large slip followed by a series of progressively smaller delays.

To me, with my original training in geophysics, this pattern looks a lot like an earthquake. Stress gradually builds up as tectonic plates move. Finally the rocks break, give off a loud bang, and settle into a less strained position. Then a series of aftershocks releases any residual stress. So it was with our projects. For a long time, people could ignore the small setbacks and minor slippages, perhaps hoping to make up the time later. Finally, as the end date loomed, they could no longer avoid reality. So they'd take a big slip to release all the built-up delay. Then the stress would build up again, and they'd take a series of smaller slips to release it.

We monitored this pattern as we continued our reviews. After a couple of years, the pattern of slips looked like Figure S1.3. Projects were still slipping. The general pattern of those slips was still pretty much the same. But the slips were happening about three months earlier in the project lifecycle. There were several reasons for this: people were monitoring status more closely; project managers could use the review team to back their judgement as to when a slip was needed, so had confidence to make the call earlier; we'd got better at defining clear milestones. Overall, however, we were simply having a much

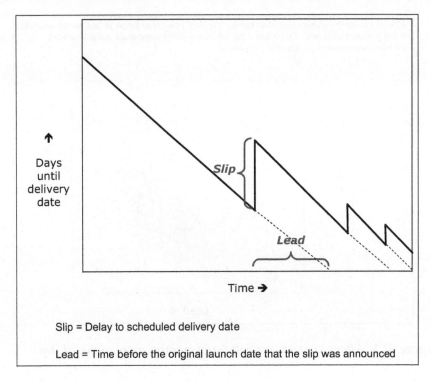

Figure S1.1 A typical project at the games company

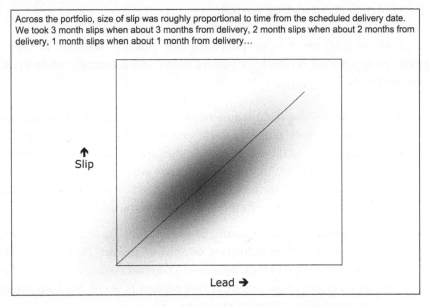

Figure S1.2 Slip was roughly proportional to time from delivery

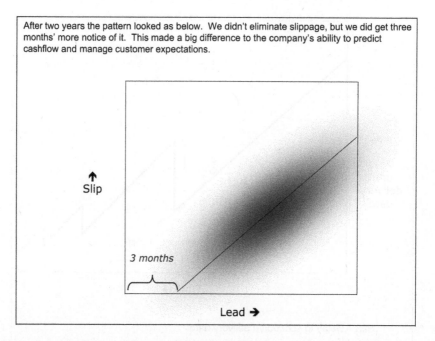

After two years the pattern looked as below. We didn't eliminate slippage, but we did get three months' more notice of it. This made a big difference to the company's ability to predict cashflow and manage customer expectations.

Figure S1.3 After two years we had three months' more notice of slip

more informed dialogue about our projects. This helped us to identify and relieve the stresses earlier. Which in turn meant that the CFO could be a little more confident about making payroll.

Of course, life's never as simple as the case studies make out. In order to operate effectively, the review team needed to overcome a number of challenges. For example:

- Game development teams have a diverse skillset – programmers, graphic artists, musicians, and so on. It can be difficult for a reviewer to understand the status of everything these specialists are working on. By doing small, frequent reviews we could get a good feel for overall trends, but sometimes we needed to call on technical experts from other teams to help us understand the details.

- Reviewers could become isolated. They floated across many teams rather than belonging to any one project. Furthermore, they sometimes had to back their own judgement against the convictions of an entire project team. So we needed to build our own internal mentoring and support structure.

- Everyone wanted to be the first to see our reports. Project managers naturally wanted a chance to fix any issues on their projects before we reported them more widely. The project managers' line management wanted to know what we were saying before their executive management heard it. And, of course, the executives we reported to wanted to hear of any issues as quickly as possible. We had to evolve clear communication protocols to win everyone's buy in.

Over time, I've come to realize that not all of life is like games development. Industries have different drivers. Companies have different strategies and approaches. People differ in all sorts of ways. I believe project reviews can add value in virtually all circumstances, but you need to tailor them to the situation. This book contains what I've learnt about tailoring and conducting reviews.

Project Success; Project Failure

Projects fail.

Our organizations invest in project management. We train project managers. We adopt project management processes. We look to organizations such as the Project Management Institute (PMI) and the UK-based Association for Project Management (APM) for support and guidance. A wealth of project management methods, bodies of knowledge, accreditations, maturity models, and so on, have been produced and eagerly taken up by practitioners and their employers and clients.

Yet projects still fail.

This is not because project managers are evil or lazy. It's not because organizations don't care about projects, nor because project teams don't want to succeed. Projects are hard. By definition, projects are about non-routine activities. Many of them are large and complex. They may involve many people, often from different backgrounds and increasingly with different languages and cultures. Complex and rapidly changing technology may be critical to success. Budgets are never large enough. There is never enough time. In amongst all this, it is easy for people to get lost, to overlook important trends, to misunderstand each other. So projects fail.

Does this matter? A certain amount of failure is probably inevitable. After all, lack of failure is a sign of lack of ambition. The problem lies in the scale of the failure.

THE COST OF PROJECT FAILURE

The best known studies of project failure, at least in the information technology (IT) industry where I specialize, are the Chaos Reports. These have been produced by the Standish Group each year since 1994. The first report (Standish

Group, 1995) estimated that 175,000 IT application development projects were undertaken in 1994, representing a total investment of US$250 billion. Only 16 per cent of those projects were considered fully successful. Of the remainder, 53 per cent ran over budget, on average spending about twice the originally budgeted cost. Even then they often delivered less than they'd planned. The remaining 31 per cent were cancelled before they'd completed.

That's an awful lot of failure.

Things are at least improving. In the 2006 survey (Standish Group, 2006), only 19 per cent of projects were cancelled before they'd completed; 35 per cent succeeded. The average cost overrun on the remaining projects was only about 60 per cent. That's better, but it still represents a vast cost to our organizations, both in wasted development funds and in foregone opportunities.

Outside the IT industry, the percentages may be different. They may even be better. However, every industry can find plenty of horror stories. Look at the construction of Wembley Stadium in London, or the Scottish Parliament, for example, or even the estimation skills of the typical builder. (The percentages may not be that different either. Consider the UK Channel 4 *Grand Designs* property makeover TV programme (Channel 4) on a dozen projects with an average budget of £225,000, the average cost overrun was 60 per cent.)

These statistics are subject to a number of challenges. Rigorously gathering survey data is expensive, so surveys often suffer from methodological weaknesses and selection biases. Many organizations are reluctant to wash their dirty linen in public, so we don't hear about some failures. Conversely, newspapers tend to focus on the big failures, so we don't hear about many successes. Analysts sell their reports by finding newsworthy results, exacerbating this latter bias.

Likewise, the statistics are very sensitive to the definition of success. Is the budget set when someone first sketches out a bright idea on the back of an envelope, or do you baseline from the (probably larger) figure that results from a few weeks of analysis? Say you set up a six month project with a budget of £1 million and projected benefits of £2 million. After a month of detailed analysis, your team comes back to you and says 'We've found a way to generate £6 million of benefits, but the project is going to take twice as long and cost twice as much.' By Standish's definition, this is a failure: it's 100 per cent over budget. But maybe from your perspective tripling your initial investment is better than doubling it? It all depends on how time-critical the end result is, and what cash you have available to invest.

Nonetheless, no-one really challenges the underlying message. Delayed, underperforming and failed projects represent a tremendous cost for many organizations. This cost comes in many guises. There is the money invested in cancelled projects. There is the cost of failing to bring new products to market. There is the cost of running inefficient operations while waiting for projects to deliver promised improvements to processes and systems. And so on.

These projects also create a tremendous personal cost for project team members, managers, sponsors and other stakeholders. People work long hours as they attempt to recover failing projects. They put other aspects of their lives on hold. Their careers are damaged by association with failure.

THE IMPORTANCE OF PROJECTS

Even if our success rate is improving, as some of the surveys suggest, it's not obvious that these costs are declining. Many organizations are doing more projects.

It's hard to gather clear statistics on this growth. Associations such as the PMI and APM can measure growth in their membership and in the number of accreditations they give out. Does this mean we're doing more projects, or simply that we've become better at promoting project management as a profession? Probably a combination of the two. Likewise, the increasing number of articles on project management published in the business literature suggests that organizations see more need to manage projects effectively, as does the proliferation of organizational maturity frameworks such as the Portfolio, Programme and Project Management Maturity Model (P3M3 – Office of Government Commerce (OGC), 2006) and the Organizational Project Maturity Model (OPM3 – PMI, 2003). This is probably driven by the increasing amounts they are investing in projects. Methodologies such as PRINCE2 (OGC, 2005) also note that organizations are dealing with an accelerating rate of change and hence need to do more projects to handle it. Finally, studies such as Wheatley (2005) confirm the trend, but find it difficult to quantify.

Let's take this on faith for now. Organizations are doing more, and more complex, projects. That certainly accords with my experience, and that of many people I've spoken to. A couple of factors lie at the heart of this.

For a start, projects are a way of implementing change. They help us build new processes, new structures, new products, and so on. In a rapidly changing world, the ability to change effectively is an increasingly important strategic capability. The ability to execute projects is part of this capability.

Second, we've done many of the easy projects. Where it used to be good enough simply to be able to schedule our fleet of trucks efficiently, we now need to coordinate a supply chain that spreads across many organizations and several continents. Where a simple customer database used to be all we desired, we now need a suite of analytical tools and increasingly flexible business processes to use their results. Where it used to be good enough to deliver individual projects on time and on budget, many organizations are finding that they need to optimize a complex portfolio of projects and programmes in order to compete.

If we are doing more projects, and these projects are increasingly complex, then it's entirely feasible that the cost of failure is growing even as we get better. We need to get better even faster.

PROJECTS, PROGRAMMES, PORTFOLIOS

Before I go too much further, I need to address some points of terminology. First, does this discussion only apply to projects, or is it relevant to programmes too? What's the difference between the two?

Here are some working definitions (from APM, 2006):

- A project is 'a unique, transient endeavour undertaken to achieve a desired outcome'.

- A programme is 'a group of related projects, which may include business-as-usual activities, that together achieve a beneficial change of a strategic nature for an organization'.

- A portfolio is 'a grouping of projects, programmes and other activities carried out under the sponsorship of an organization'.

To some people, these definitions are contentious. Different organizations and associations have slightly different definitions. There's a grey area between projects and programmes: initiatives can look like programmes from one perspective (of a particular business unit, for example), yet only like individual projects from another perspective (of senior executives or of other business units). For other people, the difference is irrelevant – projects or programmes are simply part of the wider spectrum of activities we undertake in order to deliver on our mission.

I'm not going to engage in this debate. The above definitions are 'good enough' for me to work with. What I care about is how we can use projects and programmes to deliver our organizational objectives more effectively, and in particular what role reviews and assurance play in doing this. That brings me to my second point of terminology. What do I mean by reviews and assurance?

I take my working definition of assurance from OGC, 2004a:

> Assurance is '[i]ndependent assessment and confirmation that the programme as a whole or any of its aspects are on track, applying relevant practices and procedures, and that the projects, activities and business rationale remain aligned to the programme's objectives'.

We conduct assurance by looking at the project or programme and identifying ways in which it could be improved. That is, by performing reviews. (My *Shorter Oxford English Dictionary* defines 'review' as 'the act of looking over something, with a view to improvement or correction'.)

In most cases, when I talk about processes, techniques or considerations that apply to project reviews, they apply equally well to programme and portfolio reviews. If there's a material difference, then I'll try to call attention to it. Otherwise, in places where I talk about 'projects', it's safe to assume I was just too lazy to write 'projects and/or programmes'.

THE ROLE OF REVIEWS

Two things are clear to me when I consider the role of reviews and assurance in delivering our organizations' objectives. First, any initiative, whether project, programme or portfolio, needs clear and validated information about its objectives, status, risks, and so on, in order to succeed. Reviews play an important part in delivering that information.

Second, there are many different ways to run a review. The best approach for any specific review depends on the circumstances. Differences in organizational objectives, processes and culture all influence our approach to reviews. Two organizations may approach the same project in very different ways, and for good reasons. The differences in the resulting project organizations and approaches may be far greater than the difference between a 'project' and a 'programme' within either organization alone. You need to account for these differences when setting up and performing a review.

That said, we shouldn't get hung up on the differences. The similarities between organizations are also pretty striking. They're all staffed by people, after all. It is possible to find principles and practices with general applicability.

Some purists out there have probably already discounted this book on the basis that I'm not rigorously separating projects and programmes in my thinking. For the rest of you, I hope I can help explore some of those common principles and practices, and work out how to identify and handle the differences.

THE IMPORTANCE OF INFORMATION

Whatever we call them, we need to do our projects better. I believe that the key to this is information. If we don't know how our projects are doing, then we can't act to keep them on course. It's as simple as that.

The Chaos Reports affirm this. They attribute much of the improvement in project success rates over the last decade or so to iterative development approaches. Regular iterations mean we have clear checkpoints on project status. They make it easier to test how we're doing as we proceed. They create visibility. Project reviews and assurance are another means for doing the same thing.

Such information is important for other reasons too. For a start, the cost of doing projects poorly extends beyond individual projects. Lack of clean information on an individual project's status makes it difficult to allocate resources effectively across a portfolio. Without information, we can't prioritize effectively. We can't predict resource contention. We can't identify and address risks that cut across several projects. Project reviews and assurance provide information that is vital to effective portfolio management.

For many organizations, this problem affects their corporate governance. As organizations do more projects, an increasing proportion of their assets becomes tied up in the project portfolio. Project finance, staffing, systems – they all become part of a pool of intellectual 'work in progress' that is analogous to the stockpiles of parts that used to litter factory floors before lean manufacturing came into vogue. This work in progress now constitutes a material portion of many organizations' assets. As such, they need accurate information on its status and disposition so that they can manage it effectively, and so that they can report on it to their shareholders, regulators and other stakeholders. With this in mind, project assurance functions need to work closely with audit teams, and take legislation, such as Sarbanes Oxley, into account.

Finally, there's an opportunity cost associated with weak information. If we lack information, or don't have confidence in the information we do have, then it becomes harder to manage risk. Without clean information, we avoid taking risks that are otherwise quite manageable. How many worthwhile projects do we avoid doing simply because we can't be confident they'll be delivered effectively? For some organizations, almost paralysed by these uncertainties, effective project reviews could make it possible to take on some very valuable projects.

REASONS FOR PROJECT FAILURE

So, what sort of information do we need from our project reviews? To answer this, we need to explore what's going wrong with our projects.

There's been a lot written about project failure. Organizations such as the Standish Group and the UK's OGC (e.g. OGC, 2002, 2004b, 2006) identify causes such as:

- The link between project and organizational objectives is unclear, or becomes broken as circumstances change.

- Success criteria, scope and requirements are unclear or unrealistic.

- Senior managers fail to take ownership of the project, or to provide clear leadership and direction.

- The project team fails to engage effectively with users and other external stakeholders (or vice versa).

- There is a lack of key skills or resources.

- Schedules and plans are unrealistic.

- The project team fails to operate as a cohesive unit, with clear allocation of roles and responsibilities.

- The capabilities of suppliers, technologies and tools are mis-estimated, especially in the face of a rapidly changing marketplace.

- There is a failure to perform key processes, such as communications, risk management, quality management, change management and benefits realization, effectively.

- There is a failure to break the project down into manageable steps.

- There is a failure to effectively track progress and to intervene when the project gets off course.

To put it another way, to avoid project failures we need clear information in a number of areas:

- Objectives: Are they appropriate and realistic?

- Stakeholders: Do all stakeholders (executives, sponsors, project team, and so on) have a clear and common understanding of their objectives, success criteria, roles and responsibilities?

- Resources: What roles, skills, resources and time are necessary to deliver the project, and how well do the available resources match this profile?

- Processes: Do we have the appropriate processes in place? Are they being followed? Are they delivering the expected results?

- Performance: How well are our teams, tools and suppliers actually performing? Are their actions taking us towards our objectives? Are they doing this in an effective and efficient manner?

Above all, we need a clear picture of where we are at any point in time, and of how well this matches our expected progress.

THIS BOOK

So here, in a nutshell, is my thesis.

In a complex and rapidly changing world, organizations need to evolve in order to survive. Projects are a key mechanism through which they do this. At best, then, failed projects impose enormous costs on our organizations. At worst, they threaten their very survival.

We know a lot about the causes of project failure. Our project management bodies of knowledge are full of good advice on how to prevent or mitigate these causes. We have developed mechanisms for propagating this knowledge

– professional bodies, certifications, methodologies. People and organizations have invested heavily in these mechanisms. Yet projects still fail.

Good project management is necessary, but it's not enough. Outstanding project managers can manage upwards (their sponsor) and outwards (other stakeholders) as well as managing their team. But even they have trouble keeping on top of all the information that characterizes a typical project in today's environment. Likewise, sponsors, teams and other stakeholders find it difficult to see exactly what's happening on their projects. And if they can't see what's going on, they can't discharge their roles effectively.

Project reviews and assurance help these people to understand what's really going on with their projects. However, in order for reviews and assurance to provide this information, we need to perform them effectively. This book explores some of the things we need to think about in order to perform effective project reviews and assurance.

Chapter 2 looks at different types of project review. It discusses common trade-offs we need to consider when setting up a review or assurance pro- gramme. It then identifies three key challenges to running such a programme: the difficulty of running reviews themselves; the difficulty of getting people to act on their findings; and the difficulty of embedding a sustainable review process into an organization.

Part II of this book then looks at the first of these challenges. Chapters 3 and 4 set out a process model for project reviews. This model identifies some of the parameters governing execution of reviews. A clear understanding of these parameters can help people set up reviews more effectively. Chapter 5 looks at the feedback loops in the model, and particularly at how these feedbacks can be used to enhance organizational learning.

Chapters 6 and 7 then look at some of the more pragmatic details of performing reviews. If the primary purpose of reviews is to deliver clear and validated information, evidence gathering is at the core of reviewing. Chapter 6 therefore looks in more detail at some of the techniques we use for evidence gathering. Chapter 7 looks at logistics. Scheduling meetings, keeping records, managing checklists – these may not seem very exciting, but they can overwhelm review teams if they're not handled effectively.

Part III looks at the second challenge to performing effective reviews: getting people to act on their findings. In order to deliver actionable findings, reviewers need to understand who is able to take what action within their organizations. This is the realm of governance. Chapter 8 develops a simple model to help understand how reviews and assurance relate to project and programme governance. Chapter 9 extends this model to consider how assurance fits into broader organizational governance.

Finally, Part IV of this book looks at the challenges of setting up a review or assurance programme within an organization. It views these challenges from two perspectives. Chapter 10 considers organizational change management. It examines some of the issues you may need to address as you persuade executives, managers and project teams to adopt reviews. Chapter 11 considers the issues of managing an independent review or assurance team. If organizations have trouble coping with reviews, review teams can also have trouble coping with organizations. How might you manage the stresses that result?

THE CASE STUDIES

The core of this book is built around some models of project review processes and governance. The models have been derived from practice, so I have interspersed examples of review practices between the chapters. These case studies have been drawn from practitioners, project management literature and from practices in other industries. They are intended to illustrate the range of types of review that people conduct, the sort of benefits they derive from these reviews, and the type of challenges they deal with as they execute them.

None of these case studies is 'right' or 'wrong' or 'best practice' or 'bad practice'. They're simply examples of the ways that people are doing things in a range of different circumstances. They may help you take the more conceptual material in the main chapters and apply it to your circumstances. I suggest you treat this as a learning process: try something, review how well it's working, then refine and improve.

The following case studies and examples have been included:

- *Earthquakes in the Project Portfolio*: Describes some of my experiences of running an independent assurance team in the games industry. We used a combination of gateways and regular, lightweight project reviews to track project status and improve the predictability of delivery.

- *Formal Gateways in the Public Sector*: Describes the Gateway™ reviews overseen by the UK's OGC. These are one of the best documented examples of project reviews, and illustrate the benefits of a well-defined and formal review programme.

- *Lessons from Problems in the Past*: Describes one organization's experience of using quality reviews to share lessons and expertise across teams in the oil industry.

- *Post-Project Reviews and Retrospectives*: Discusses techniques for project retrospectives and related reviews. Again, these can be a useful way to capture lessons and share them within an organization.

- *Weeding the Project Portfolio*: Goes back to my experience in the games industry. Out of control projects can waste a lot of resources. They can also be very hard to kill. This case study looks at the traps this can create for review teams.

- *Assuring Fixed Price Implementations*: Looks at how a professional services firm combines peer reviews, gateways and health checks to ensure that it consistently delivers fixed price projects to time and budget.

- *Programme Reviews in a Merged Environment*: Discusses the use of project reviews to bring stability and a shared project management culture following a merger between two corporations.

- *Software Review and Inspection Techniques*: Project reviewers can learn from software engineering, where the literature describes several techniques, of varying degrees of formality, for conducting software quality reviews. This study gives a brief overview of these techniques.

- *Review Techniques in the Education Sector*: Much research has been done into techniques for reviewing the effectiveness of teaching. School inspections are a well-established, if politically sensitive, practice. What can project reviewers learn from these practices?

- *Assuring Quality in a Global Application Portfolio*: Examines one company's use of reviews to improve communications across globally distributed teams. By clarifying assumptions about requirements and quality attributes, reviews help such teams overcome the issues of geographical, organizational and cultural boundaries.

- *Completion Bonds in the Film Industry*: Film financiers often demand insurance for their investments, guaranteeing that their money will be repaid if the film is not produced to the original budget and schedule. Assurance processes play an important role for the insurance companies providing these bonds.

These case studies touch on some of the dimensions that need to be considered when setting up a review or assurance programme. How should we balance our effort between regular, small reviews versus less frequent but more formal gate reviews? Are there advantages to using independent specialists to conduct reviews, or would it be better to simply ask project managers to review their peers' projects? Should we focus on reviewing the technical quality of deliverables, or on overall business objectives and project status? Figures 1.1 and 1.2 illustrate where each case study lies on these dimensions. Chapter 2 discusses these issues in more detail.

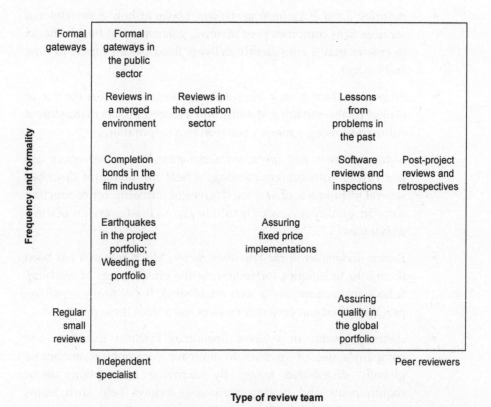

Figure 1.1 Case studies by frequency and formality

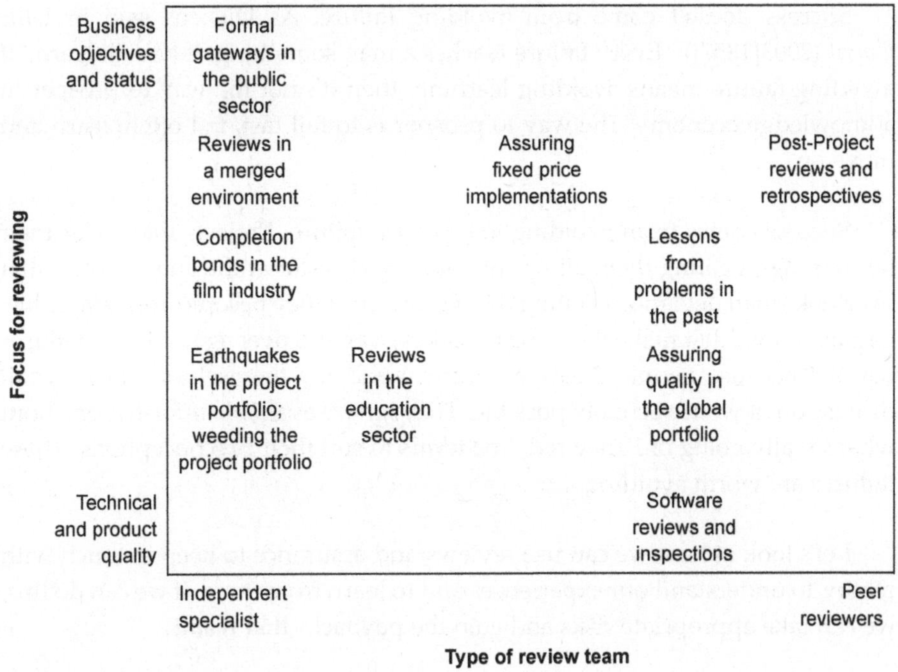

Business objectives and status

Focus for reviewing

Formal gateways in the public sector			
Reviews in a merged environment	Assuring fixed price implementations		Post-Project reviews and retrospectives
Completion bonds in the film industry		Lessons from problems in the past	
Earthquakes in the project portfolio; weeding the project portfolio	Reviews in the education sector	Assuring quality in the global portfolio	
		Software reviews and inspections	

Technical and product quality

Independent specialist

Peer reviewers

Type of review team

Figure 1.2   Case studies by reviewing focus

AVOIDING UNNECESSARY FAILURE

One final thought before we launch into this journey. A large industry has grown up around project failure. People perform research into its prevalence and causes. They develop ways to address these causes: bodies of knowledge, certifications, processes, and so on. They write books (like this one!). They sell consulting, methodologies and tools.

This industry has produced a lot statistics and reports, some of them well researched and unbiased. It has produced a lot of good advice on how to avoid failure. However, there is one thing it rarely tells you. It's easy to avoid project failures. Just don't do any projects.

The fact is that a certain amount of failure is inevitable if we are going to change and innovate. Whenever we try to do new things, we're going to get it wrong at least occasionally. Sometimes we'll do very risky projects because they have a high potential payback. Only one in eight exploration wells drilled in the North Sea discovered economic deposits of oil or gas. Yet those successes more than paid for the seven in eight 'failures'.

Success doesn't come from avoiding failure. As Dickens said in *Little Dorrit* (2003[1857]): 'Every failure teaches a man something, if he will learn.' If avoiding failure means avoiding learning, then it's not the way to prosper in a knowledge economy. The way to prosper is to fail fast, fail often, learn and move on.

Success comes from avoiding *unnecessary* failure. Projects that cover their failures, aggregating them all up into one big disaster at the end. Projects that overlook small deviations, letting them grow until they become unmanageable. Organizations that make the same mistakes over and over again. These failures happen because people create a dream world for themselves. They curtail discussion of what's actually possible. They ignore available information about what's really going on. They redefine terms to suit their preconceptions. These failures are worth avoiding.

Let's look at how we can use reviews and assurance to keep in touch with reality, to understand our experiences and to learn from them. If we can do this, we can take appropriate risks and gain the paybacks that result.

Project Reviews

FACING REALITY

As we saw in Chapter 1, projects fail for many reasons: optimistic estimates; technology that doesn't work as advertised; misunderstanding the needs of key stakeholders; plans driven by deadlines rather than feasibility; teams' belief that, given enough pizza, they can solve any problem by tomorrow morning.

In my experience, many of these reasons come back to one root cause: people lose touch with reality. For example:

- We spend insufficient time exploring assumptions at the start of a project, so people operate from different expectations of what's required or how they'll work together. This makes it almost impossible to build meaningful estimates and schedules. The project begins from a position of unrealistic expectations and is playing catch-up forever after.

- We set out with an over-optimistic assessment of our team's capabilities, or of the technology and methodologies we're using. Initial slow progress is put down to lack of familiarity. Eventually the reality of slower than expected progress hits us.

- Sponsors may not realize (another word rooted in reality) how much effort and commitment they need to put into sponsorship, or what skills will be required. They may assume that the project manager can handle many of the things that are properly their responsibility. A project with weak leadership will then have trouble connecting to broader organizational objectives.

- We negotiate poorly with key stakeholders. How often have you seen an executive beat down the initial estimate from a technical team? The team thinks they're estimating, but the executive is conducting a negotiation. Someone's lost touch with reality.

- Busy teams find it difficult to step back and think about what's really going on. Minor deviations accumulate because everyone has their nose to the grindstone and can't see the underlying trend.

- Even if we can see the underlying trend, we have trouble reporting it. A culture that says 'come to me with solutions, not problems' may mean that unsolved problems don't get talked about. A culture where senior managers are expected to have all the answers may mean that sponsors can't admit it that they don't understand what their project manager is saying. Often people just don't know who to go to with their observations. So people with problems have trouble connecting to people who may have solutions, and the project's leadership remains disconnected from the real situation.

- And, of course, many of us don't even want to think about what the real risks might be.

This doesn't happen because people are lazy, or because they are trying to sabotage their projects. Skills and experience may provide some insulation, but they don't eliminate the problems completely. People lose touch with reality for reasons rooted in basic psychology. The next sections discuss some of these reasons. (See also Ullman, 2006 or Virine and Trumper, 2007)

OVERCONFIDENCE

People tend to overestimate their own ability. Surveys show, for example, that most people consider themselves to be of above average intelligence, or to be better drivers than average. Likewise, most consultancies and systems integrators claim a significantly higher success rate than the industry average.

This overconfidence is a direct cause of underestimation on some projects. It can also lead to issues such as scope creep (people think they can implement a new feature with little effort) and the 90 per cent complete syndrome. (People report that they are nearly finished because they genuinely believe they only have one or two small things to fix. Sometimes they believe this for weeks on end.)

OVERSIMPLIFICATION

People tend to use simplifying assumptions and mental models in order to deal with complexity. This is sometimes essential, for example where rapid decision making is important, but it can also lead to traps. Most of us have been caught by time, cost and complexity estimates that escalate as we get further into the details ('the devil's in the details'). Yet we still start our projects with broad, 'high level' estimates.

Likewise, we often operate from mental models for how projects, teams or organizations should work. These are simplifications of reality; they embed large numbers of assumptions. If we use them unthinkingly, we fail to recognize situations where the assumptions are violated. We begin to operate in model land rather than the real world. (Smith (2007) examines some of the assumptions behind the project management paradigm.)

When we fail to recognize the true complexity of our projects, their requirements and the organizations that they are serving, we accept unrealistic scope, estimates, staffing and plans. We also fail to recognize and manage key risks.

AVOIDING PAIN

People tend to avoid pain. Sometimes this means deferring immediate pain at the risk (or even certainty) of needing to deal with greater future pain. For example, rather than face up to a tough conversation now ('it probably can't be done'), we take high-risk options ('the only way it can be done is if we cut all these corners and hope nothing goes wrong'). Likewise, rather than going through the pain of admitting that we've been delayed, we find reasons to persuade ourselves that we'll catch up by the next milestone.

The pain we're avoiding comes from a variety of sources:

- We may be avoiding confrontation, anger or disappointment. This is why many people have trouble saying 'no' – they'd rather fail later than deal with anger or disappointment now.

- We may be avoiding the feeling of loss of control or mastery. People may focus on tasks that they're good at, rather than those that are important. Technical people often derive a lot of their identity from their ability to solve problems – admitting they can't solve a problem represents a deep threat to their sense of identity. Managers who like to feel in control of the situation may avoid finding out about things they can't control. (Of course, not knowing about it means they definitely can't control it.)

- We may be avoiding cultural taboos, with consequent fears of ostracism and the like. Some teams and cultures find it difficult to say 'no' for this reason – there are strong cultural pressures to make 'positive' responses. Many organizations find it difficult to discuss risks for a similar reason – there's a strong pressure to 'smile, it may never happen'.

- We may be avoiding loss of 'face'. For example, senior managers often find it difficult to admit their ignorance to the people reporting to them. Rather than seek clarification to status reports, they may allow things to drift. (This is a common reason for weak project sponsorship: the sponsor simply doesn't know how to help, and doesn't want to ask. Strong project managers can manage their sponsors, but more inexperienced project managers, who are most likely to need support, can find this difficult to negotiate.)

- We may be avoiding apparent costs. Spending time to clarify objectives; allocating resources to risk mitigation activities; undertaking further analysis of the problem; performing independent reviews and assurance – these all involve immediate costs, often with uncertain paybacks. There is often a strong pressure to avoid these immediate, obvious costs in order to reduce budgets.

For whatever reason, these behaviours act to shield us from reality. As often as not, we are deferring pain rather than avoiding it. Our projects suffer in the end.

CONFIRMATION BIAS

People tend to look for evidence that confirms their existing hopes and beliefs. We want, for example, to believe that our project is on course so we seek evidence that shows we are hitting milestones, and ignore information that shows where we're behind schedule. As a team makes commitments to budgets, estimates, schedules and deliverables, this bias becomes more embedded – they begin to focus their energy on finding ways to achieve these commitments and to avoid any signs of problems or risks. (The reverse can also be true – once a team begins to believe the project will fail, they focus their energy on seeking reasons why it will fail.) Again, this bias acts to shield us from uncomfortable realities.

Confirmation bias is often built into our project approval processes. People say what they think they need to say in order to get the projects they believe in approved. They may not lie, but they focus on the positive aspects of the project and pay only cursory attention to the costs, risks and side effects. This then becomes the approved version of the project's storyline, to become embedded in people's thinking through repetition.

REPETITION BIAS

If people hear a message often enough, they begin to believe it. This is the basis of most marketing and propaganda. Eventually, we may end up believing our own propaganda – a team takes initial, rough estimates and works with them, gradually losing sight of the fact that there's little basis behind them; a manager repeats the high-level vision to all who will listen and starts to mistake the vision for delivered reality.

This happens within our suppliers too. Vendors rarely lie about the capabilities of their tools, for example. They genuinely believe what they're saying. They hear their own marketing messages so often, however, that they begin to forget about the gaps and weaknesses. This rosy view then feeds into our own estimation of their capabilities.

PERCEPTUAL BIASES

People often find it harder to recognize gradual trends than sudden changes. Or else we get locked into our view of individual details rather than seeing the bigger picture. In the words of Fred Brooks (Brooks, 1995): 'How does a project get to be a year late? One day at a time.' When we're under pressure, we see those days as individual, disconnected events and lose track of the bigger trend towards disaster. These and similar biases cause us to overlook key information.

REINFORCEMENT LOOPS

These biases often combine and reinforce each other. We want to believe that we're above average at what we do, so confirmation bias reinforces our overconfidence. As we continue to confirm how good we are, repetition bias adds further reinforcement. This growing overconfidence makes us more prone to use pain-avoidance strategies – we assume we'll be able to solve any problems, so don't face up to potential difficulties or invest in analysis and risk mitigation.

ORGANIZATIONAL ACCELERATORS

Finally, organizational dynamics and culture can compound these tendencies to lose touch with reality. Organizations that focus on apportioning blame rather than correcting problems increase the pain associated with admitting difficulties, increasing the chances that people will hide them. Likewise, very hierarchical organizations can exacerbate the pain associated with confrontation or loss of face, making it difficult for people at different levels to admit their uncertainties to each other. Conversely, collegial cultures exacerbate the risks of 'groupthink', the tendency for people in a group to converge on consensus at the expense of critical examination. In such situations, overconfidence and confirmation biases can easily prevail.

Projects that span organizational boundaries face additional challenges. This is especially true in complex joint ventures and outsourcing relationships that involve multiple organizations, but it also affects projects working across group and unit boundaries within a single organization. People may be uncertain as to what information can be shared or how it should be shared. Different professional backgrounds, languages and conventions may make it difficult to fully understand the information that is shared. Contracts and legal concerns can create further barriers – penalty clauses, for example, may help align objectives across organizations, but they also create incentives to hide issues. Procurement regulations may restrict what information can be shared at key stages in the project. All these barriers can make it harder for people to uncover and deal with the above cognitive biases.

For projects to succeed in these circumstances, they need to find ways to break through these dynamics and bring reality into view.

CRUNCH

Underlying all this, reality doesn't always give us the message we want to hear. We don't want to hear that we're less intelligent than we'd like, or less capable of solving problems, or that we code too slowly. Project failure is one of the prices we pay to avoid (or at least delay) hearing these messages.

Eventually, however, our projects come face-to-face with reality: something happens that means we can no longer avoid it. Unfortunately, by the time this happens it's often too late. Our Project Management Bodies of Knowledge (PMBOKs) and methodologies and lifecycle models are full of good advice. They provide many tools to help us map out our expectations and to monitor actual progress against these expectations. But these tools can only be used if people can overcome their tendencies to ignore unpleasant facts.

This is where project reviews come in. They are a way to help people (teams, project managers, sponsors, other stakeholders) manage these human biases and keep in touch with what's really happening on their projects. (They are not the only way. They work in conjunction with testing and quality assurance, with status reporting and earned value calculations, with many of the techniques of agile development – information radiators and pair programming, for example. My experience is that reviews are an invaluable part of this toolkit, however.)

THE ROLE OF PROJECT REVIEWS

The primary purpose of project reviews, then, is to ground people in reality. By providing clear and independently validated information to project stakeholders, reviews help people avoid cognitive biases and information bottlenecks such as those described above.

Of course, projects typically have many stakeholders, with diverse information needs. The specific objectives for any individual review will focus on a subset of these. Table 2.1 illustrates some of the stakeholders that reviews can support, and the types of information these stakeholders may be interested in.

This matrix is illustrative: stakeholder roles and needs vary widely across different organizations and projects. For example, portfolio management and project support offices vary widely in their remits and hence their information needs. Or executives may take great interest in the details of strategic projects. When setting up a review or assurance process, you will need to map out this landscape and hence identify how reviews can add most value for your particular circumstances.

Parts III and IV of this book will come back to this question. In general, however, project managers and teams need detailed insight into the project's status and performance so they can manage it effectively. Sponsors need a broader overview of the project so they can manage its commitments with the wider organization. Executives need information to help them prioritize and manage their investments across their portfolio of projects and other activities. And people depending on a project's outputs need a realistic assessment of whether it will deliver what they are expecting, so that they can make decisions about their own work (e.g. whether to invoke contingency plans).

Reviews can help in several ways beyond this core role of providing independently validated information. For a start, reviewers can help people to understand the information. Sponsors, for example, are often not project management professionals: they may not fully understand the terminology or implications of status reports and other messages they receive. They can also be overwhelmed by the amount of information they receive. Reviewers can help sponsors and other executives to understand this information, prioritize it

Table 2.1   Reviews can provide information to diverse stakeholders

	Project managers and teams	Project and programme sponsors	Portfolio managers	Project management/support offices	Executive management	Auditors	Managers of units dependent on project outputs
Project Objectives							
Are project objectives aligned to organizational objectives?	O	✓	✓		O	O	O
Is the business case well founded, and is the project still aligned to it?	✓	✓	✓		O	O	
Do all stakeholders have common understanding of the project's objectives?	✓	O					
Are these objectives realistic?	✓	✓	O		O		
Stakeholders							
Are roles and responsibilities clearly defined, and does everyone understand them?	✓	O					
Do people have clear success criteria?	✓	O					
Does the project team understand the requirements?	✓	O					O
Is the project team communicating effectively internally?	✓	O		✓			
Is the project team communicating effectively with external stakeholders?	✓	✓	O	✓	O		✓
Resources							
Is the budget and schedule realistic?	✓	O	O			O	
Are the necessary skills and resources in place?	✓	O	O			O	
Does this project represent the best way to invest organizational resources?		O	✓		✓	O	
Processes							
Are plans and schedules being managed effectively?	✓	O		✓		O	
Are risks being identified and managed effectively?	✓	O		✓		O	
Are changes being managed effectively?	✓	O		✓		O	
Is quality being managed effectively?	✓	O		✓		O	
Are appropriate controls in place (e.g. for fraud)?	✓	O				✓	
Are there 'best practices' being developed elsewhere in the organization that the project might benefit from?	✓	O		✓		O	
Performance							
Is the project making the anticipated progress?	✓	O	O			O	O
Are costs aligned to the budget?	✓	O	O			O	
What is causing any delays and overruns?	✓	O				O	

Table 2.1   *Concluded*

	Project managers and teams	Project and programme sponsors	Portfolio managers	Project management/support offices	Executive management	Auditors	Managers of units dependent on project outputs
What are the key risks?	✓	O	O		O	O	
Is the project likely to hit its targets?	✓	O	O		O	O	✓
Are the deliverables of appropriate quality?	✓	O	O			O	✓
What might be done to improve performance?	✓	O				O	
O = Overview (Are there issues? Do I need to intervene, or is the project manager in control?) ✓ = Detailed view (Is there anything I'm overlooking? What do I need to manage?)							

and hence intervene effectively. Without this support, sponsors may either fail to intervene, leaving project managers to handle prioritization and resource contention issues that are beyond their authority, or intervene too closely, micromanaging the project.

Reviewers can also facilitate dialogue between stakeholders. Project teams often have trouble communicating key messages to senior executives – they may lack the credibility or breadth of perspective to frame their messages effectively, for example. Reviewers are well placed to help. Similarly, by identifying where misunderstandings are happening and why, reviewers can help diverse stakeholders to build a common language and understanding of project objectives, status, roles, and so on. When reviewers make it clear that they are interested primarily in clarity of information, and not in underlying agendas, their role as trusted facilitators can be extremely valuable.

Review and assurance teams are also well placed to help connect projects to wider organizational objectives. As they work across a portfolio of projects, they are able to help individual project teams understand the broader perspective for their work.

Finally, reviews can be an important mechanism for embedding organizational learning. Many organizations struggle to disseminate lessons learned on one project to other projects in their portfolio. Likewise, project management offices and process engineering groups often struggle to persuade projects to adopt the 'best practices' they have developed. By incorporating such assets into their reference models, review teams can help project teams become aware of them and use them effectively. (I believe this role in disseminating organizational learning is one of the most important roles for project reviews. It is discussed further in Chapter 5.)

Reviews can also help personal learning. Reviewers can mentor project team members. (Both mentor and mentee gain from this – the mentee gains from the mentor's experience while the mentor gains from reflecting on that experience.) Participating in review teams can provide an opportunity for people to see and learn from a wider range of projects. Perhaps most importantly, reviews can provide space for people and teams to reflect on what they are doing.

Projects tend to be high pressure environments – people are often too rushed to sit back and think. By providing a sounding board for people to discuss their experiences and perceptions and by asking clarifying questions, reviewers can help people to think through what is really going on and hence to find their own solutions. It's remarkable how often this has happened to me, from both sides of the conversation. (It's also an indictment of the way many organizations set up projects that this space to think is so rare.)

Of course, it's hard to fulfil all of these roles at once. When setting up a review, you need to choose where to focus.

BENEFITS OF EFFECTIVE PROJECT REVIEWS

Reviews help organizations to clarify what is going on, disseminate this information and hence to learn from experience. As they do this, organizations can expect to derive benefits in two areas – execution of individual projects and overall decision making across the portfolio of projects.

The case studies give several examples of the benefits that organizations gain in project execution. These include:

- Earlier identification of risks and issues: As it often becomes more difficult, or even impossible, to rectify problems as they escalate and accumulate, this reduces project costs and failure rates. In extremis, it allows projects to be cancelled sooner, reducing the investment in failed projects.

- Adoption of good practice: Reviewers can help project teams to identify, understand and adopt practices learned from experience elsewhere in the organization.

- Availability of skills and experience: Reviewers take their experience to a range of projects, both directly and through mentoring. They also learn by seeing this range of projects, then bring this learning back to their own projects. Both mechanisms allow projects to benefit from a wider range of skills and experience than would otherwise be available. This process also builds resilience against staff turnover and associated issues, by developing a pool of people with understanding of several projects.

- Improved communication: Reviewers can help project teams to think through and make the case for the resources they need. They can help teams to engage and communicate with other stakeholders. The clarity and understanding that reviews create can significantly enhance communication within and around the project.

Reviews may also create a hidden benefit. People often put more thought into their project structure, plans, risk analyses, and so on, when they know that someone is going to review them thoroughly. This thinking can itself do much to improve project execution. (This doesn't always happen. Sometimes teams put in less effort, thinking that reviewers will find and correct any issues. Reviewers need to be aware of this risk, and call attention to it if it does happen.)

Benefits for portfolio decision making come in areas such as the following:

- Improved ability to allocate resources: Improved visibility of individual project status helps portfolio managers to prioritize and allocate resources effectively. This is especially important when resources are constrained or when there are bottlenecks on key skills.

- Improved predictability of project delivery: Improved visibility helps managers of dependent projects to plan and develop contingencies. It also increases the organization's ability to make meaningful commitments to its customers, markets and other external stakeholders.

- Greater confidence to take risks: Clearer understanding of the risks associated with each project can give organizations more confidence to take well-judged risks.

Many of these benefits can be difficult to quantify, especially if the organization does not have a well-defined baseline to measure against. When setting up an assurance programme, it's worth considering how to baseline and monitor these benefits so that investment in reviews can be balanced against other improvement efforts. We will come back to this issue in Chapter 10.

TYPES OF REVIEW

We've seen that reviews can serve a wide range of stakeholders and fulfil a variety of roles. It's therefore not surprising that organizations undertake several different types of review. APM (2006) recognizes five types of review:

1. Evaluation review: Can happen at any point through the project. It checks progress against the original schedule, budget and deliverables, and reviews the effectiveness of project management and related processes. It typically delivers some sort of assessment of the likelihood of project success and identifies areas of concern and corrective actions.

2. Gate review: Happens at the end of a project phase or at some other defined point in the project's lifecycle. It typically represents a decision point, using the outputs from an evaluation to decide whether continued investment in the project is justified.

3. Audit: An objective evaluation by a group outside the project team. (Note that, by this definition, an OGC Gateway™ review, as discussed in the case study *Formal Gateways in the Public Sector*, is an audit. The OGC insists that this isn't the case. The distinction between reviews and audits generates a lot of debate: it's discussed further below.)

4. Post-project review: Happens as the project closes down. It assesses the overall success of the project and identifies what did or didn't work during its execution, generating lessons learned for the future.

5. Benefits realization review: Happens after the organization has had some chance to use the outputs from the project. It evaluates the extent to which the benefits identified in the original business case have been achieved.

This classification focuses on when the review happens in the project lifecycle, with some attention to the degree of independence of the reviewers. Other classifications use criteria such as the degree of formality of the review (e.g. Weigers, 2002), or the attributes of the project that the review is focusing on (e.g. quality, progress or risk reviews). The next sections discuss each of these attributes in turn.

TIMING OF REVIEWS

There are essentially three options for timing reviews:

1. Event based: Reviews are timed to fall at key points in the project lifecycle. Thus, for example, gate reviews coincide with points such as the decision to initiate a procurement, sign a contract or commit to a particular design. Gates aim to ensure that people have the information they need to make these decisions. Other event-based reviews include end of iteration, end of phase and post-project reviews. These typically aim to assess how well the actual deliverables match the original intentions, how well the project team and processes have been performing, and hence to identify lessons learned and adjust plans for the next phase.

2. Periodic: Reviews happen at regular intervals throughout the project. These can range from frequent, lightweight reviews (perhaps a conference call every couple of weeks) to larger, less frequent assessments (maybe a one- or two-day session every quarter throughout a large project). These typically aim to ensure that the project team is not overlooking any issues or trends, and to provide advice and guidance. Small, frequent reviews are good at spotting trends, but may not examine the project closely enough to spot deeper issues. Larger reviews can dig deeper, but require more resources and are more disruptive of the project team, so can only be afforded at less frequent intervals. This can make it more difficult for them to identify trends as they develop. (Again, we will come back to the question of frequency of reviews in Chapter 10.)

3. Ad hoc or one-off reviews: Often called 'health checks', these are typically set up to answer specific questions about a project. Perhaps concerns about a project's approach or status have arisen, or the organization wishes to assess the impact of major changes or risk events. By their nature, ad hoc reviews cannot be planned into the project from the outset, so are likely to be disruptive to the project team.

DEGREE OF INDEPENDENCE

One reason reviews add value is that they bring outside perspective and experience to the project. Ideally, then, they might be conducted by a completely independent team. In practice, there are a number of trade-offs here, leading again to three broad options:

1. Independent assurance: An independent team from a different part of the organization (or from a different organization) undertakes reviews. This team is likely to be trained in review techniques and may even be dedicated to reviewing, working across multiple projects in a programme or portfolio. Its independence and specialist skills mean that this team is likely to perform a more rigorous evaluation. However, it may also be less interested in supporting organizational learning than a team of internal peer reviewers. There is also a risk that an adversarial relationship develops between project and review teams. Finally, external reviewers may take time to get up to speed with an organization's culture, terminology and operating model. This adds to the expense of reviews – dedicated review teams in particular are, or appear to be, relatively expensive to operate.

2. Peer review: A group of the project team's peers comes together to provide an outside view of the project, probably by taking time off from their own projects. This helps provide an independent perspective, while avoiding some of the issues of getting up to speed with local terminology and culture. Peer reviews often have a strong emphasis on sharing experiences and learning; however, they risk losing rigour: reviewers may be too embedded in the same culture and approach to see common failure modes. At worst, reviews can degenerate into an exchange of 'war stories'. It can also be difficult for peer reviewers to find time for reviews when they are juggling them with responsibilities on their own projects.

3. Self-assessment: The project team itself conducts the review, typically aided by checklists and similar tools. This brings little in the way of independent perspective, but the exercise of stepping back and reconsidering the project from the different angles suggested by a checklist can nonetheless be extremely valuable for the team.

These options represent endpoints in a spectrum rather than absolute choices. Peer reviewers can often be selected to bring a highly independent viewpoint, for example. Self-assessments are often used as the starting point for other types of review.

DEGREE OF FORMALITY

Reviews can range from informal checkpoints with the sponsor or other stakeholders to highly formal gateways or audits. Following a more formal process, with associated assets such as detailed questionnaires and checklists, tends to increase the rigour of the review and hence the likelihood that it will uncover issues. However, it also tends to increase the cost and disruption associated with the review. The software engineering literature (e.g. Gilb and Graham, 1993) has some good discussion on the benefits of formal reviews, suggesting that this expense can be well justified, at least in some circumstances. In practice, regular informal reviews can be a big aid to communication and reflection, perhaps supplemented by more formal reviews at defined points in the project.

ATTRIBUTES BEING REVIEWED

It's not possible (within bounded cost) to review every aspect of a project at the same time. A single review typically focuses on a small number of attributes drawn from categories such as:

- Objectives: Are the objectives clear, aligned to organizational objectives and well understood by all stakeholders? Does the business case still hold up?

- Status: How is the project progressing against the anticipated schedule, budget and deliverables?

- Risk: What risks does the project face? Are risks being identified and managed effectively?

- Quality: Is the project creating products of appropriate quality? Quality can itself be subdivided into a range of perspectives – do products meet the relevant technical standards? Are they acceptable to the end users?

- Process: Is the project following appropriate processes, for example for planning, status tracking, change management, risk management? (Some people debate whether you should focus on process or products. Both are relevant. Process reviews tend to be forward looking – is this project likely to produce the appropriate outputs in the future? Product reviews look at whether the outputs produced to date are appropriate, and hence how they can be improved in future.)

- Compliance. Is the project complying with organizational policies, standards and processes?

The choice of focus depends on considerations such as the position in the project lifecycle (early reviews may focus on objectives and processes, later ones on status and quality) and whether people have any specific concerns about the project.

Reviews add most value when they have clearly defined focus areas. Unfocused reviews risk investing effort on relatively unimportant issues, or failing to gather sufficient information about important concerns. At the same time, reviewers need to be alert to unexpected issues that they may uncover, and be willing to exercise judgement in prioritizing and exploring these as necessary. Part II discusses this question of defining and managing focus in more detail.

The attributes being reviewed may influence the composition of the review team and other aspects of the review. A quality review, for example, may require specialist skills. Likewise, assessing status without some understanding of quality is meaningless – delivering products on time and to budget is meaningless if they don't work. Thus, a status review either needs to assess the quality of products produced to date, or else it needs to confirm that appropriate quality checks have been performed (that is, that appropriate quality management processes are in place).

One final point: sponsors frequently ask for a 'general review of the whole project'. How do I do this without becoming unfocused? I generally find that such reviews can be reframed to focus on objectives and risks. They ask the questions: 'What are the objectives? Does everyone understand them? What could prevent this project achieving them? What actions are people taking to manage these risks?' As the review identifies specific risks, it may then drill into other attributes.

SCOPE AND STYLE

Two final aspects are worth mentioning. First, reviews can be scoped at various levels – portfolio, programme, project or individual product. This naturally influences the amount of effort needed and the level of depth that can be examined, the types of attributes that may be relevant, and so on.

Second, the education sector (see the case study *Review Techniques in the Education Sector*) makes a distinction between summative and formative evaluations. Summative evaluations focus on making external decisions about the project. (Should the organization continue to invest in it? Does it comply with organizational standards?) Formative evaluations focus on helping the project to perform better. (How can we improve risk identification? Do we need to replan?) The distinction isn't necessarily clear cut – summative evaluations are also likely to identify areas for improvement, for example. However, it can cause confusion and resistance if the overall purpose of the review, formative or summative, isn't clear to everyone.

A BALANCED PORTFOLIO OF REVIEWS

To maximize the value from any single review, then, it essentially comes down to identifying the objectives for the review and choosing the attributes, degree of formality and independence most likely to meet this objective. Part II of this book considers this question from the perspective of how objectives influence the review process. Part III considers it from the perspective of governance (who needs what information in order to make the decisions they're responsible for?).

When setting up a programme of reviews, you're likely to use a mixture of approaches – regular, formative evaluations combined with more formal gateways at key decision points, for example, with the focus shifting from objectives at the outset to status and quality as projects progress. Table 2.2 identifies the types of review used in some of the case studies.

OTHER CONSIDERATIONS

Reviews can require a significant investment of resources, especially from the review team but also from the project team. What level of investment will give the best payback? Whose budget should it come from? Are there other ways we could spend the money to achieve similar benefits?

This section looks at some of the considerations that influence how much an organization might invest in reviews and assurance.

HOW MUCH SHOULD WE INVEST?

This question comes in many guises. Which projects should we review? How thoroughly should we review them? How much should we budget for reviews overall? There is no simple answer. The appropriate level of investment depends on the degree of risk attached to each project, and on how critical the projects are to the organization's success.

Table 2.2   Example review types

Case study	Review objective	Timing	Independence	Formality	Attributes
Earthquakes in the Project Portfolio	Decide whether to invest in full production	Event-based (Gateway)	Independent	Formal	Objectives Quality
	Assess whether project would deliver as expected.	Periodic (every 2 weeks)	Independent	Informal	Status Risk
Formal Gateways in the Public Sector	Assure project is ready to progress to next stage	Event-based (Gateway)	Independent	Formal	Varies by gate
Lessons from Problems in the Past	Identify potential problems	Event-based	Peer	Relatively informal	Risk Process Quality
Post-Project Reviews and Retrospectives	Learn lessons from project and embed in future development	Event-based (end of phase)	Self-assessment	Formal (i.e. follow defined structure)	Process Quality
Assuring Fixed Price Implementation	Assess whether project is ready for handoff to offshore team	Event-based (Gateway)	Peer	Formal	Quality Process
	Identify potential problems	Periodic (every six weeks)	Peer	Informal	Risk Status
	Identify potential problems	Ad hoc (Health Check)	Independent	Formal	Varies by review
Programme Reviews in a Merged Environment	Identify why projects were failing	Ad hoc (Health Check)	Independent	Formal	Process
Software Reviews and Inspections	Identify quality issues	Varies	Varies	Varies	Quality
Assuring the Global Application Portfolio	Identify quality issues	Event-based	Peer	Reasonably formal	Objectives Quality
Completion Bonds in the Film Industry	Assess whether project would deliver as expected	Varies	Independent	Formal	Status Quality

Looking first at how to allocate resources across projects, it seems reasonable to allocate our effort in proportion to the following factors.

- Importance of the project: Projects that are consuming a large proportion of organizational resources need to be monitored more carefully. Likewise for projects that could deliver large benefits. It may be difficult to justify any investment in reviewing small, low-impact projects, beyond self-assessments by the project team itself.

- Risk level: Complex or high-risk projects are likely to benefit more from external perspective. Projects that are perceived to carry lower levels of risk may benefit from an initial evaluation to confirm that they are indeed low risk.

- Stage of the project: Errors and oversights in the early stages of a project tend to have a large impact downstream, so it makes sense to invest more in reviewing during the early stages of projects. Thus, for example, most organizations schedule their formal gateways towards the front end of the project, moving to lighter status checks as the project progresses. In the latter stages of the project, assurance activities may shift towards testing rather than review.

- Learning: Many organizations invest little if anything in retrospectives and benefits realization reviews. This robs them of significant opportunities to learn from experience. It is worth keeping some budget back for these reviews.

The OGC Gateway™ packs (OGC, 2004b and associated website OCG, 2008) include checklists for assessing the level of resource to put into reviews. These checklists will need to be tailored to your specific circumstances, but are a useful starting point.

As you allocate this investment, ensure that the project manager is aware of it. They will need to ensure that their plans and budgets incorporate, or at least link to, the review activities. You will also need to consider mechanisms for coordinating reviewers' activities across projects.

Coming to the question of how much overall to invest in reviews, I know of no generally accepted benchmark. The *Completion Bonds in the Film Industry* case study gives one useful data point: if it is worth investing 2–6 per cent of the production budget on an insurance policy that includes a strong focus on external assurance, many projects would probably benefit by investing 1–2 per cent on assurance alone. The OGC (2002, 2005) gives another data point when it recommends investing 1–3 per cent of the project budget on initial risk assessment and then an additional 2 per cent on monitoring and updating this assessment. The optimum investment might vary by industry and project type, but both these data points suggest investing 1–2 per cent of your overall project portfolio budget in external reviews and assurance.

OWNERSHIP

Who should take responsibility for making these reviews happen? Different people may be responsible for different types of review, depending on their objectives. For example, under PRINCE2 (OGC, 2005) the project board is responsible for project assurance (including business, technical and user assurance). They may delegate execution of assurance activities, but not to the project manager or team. Where members of the board lack suitable expertise, it makes sense for them to commission an independent review team to conduct gate reviews or other evaluations.

The project manager is responsible for day-to-day running and control of the project. This is likely to include quality assurance of plans, deliverables and other artefacts, status and risk tracking, and so on. The project manager may well wish to commission independent or peer reviews to support these activities.

Corporate executives also have a stake in project status and risk. Thus, they may also commission some level of independent audit or assurance beyond that being undertaken by the project board. The level will typically depend on the risk and importance associated with the project, and the degree of trust within the organization.

Finally, some approaches devolve responsibility to self-organizing project teams. Agile development methods (Schwaber, 2003; Johnson, 2006) are a good example and tend to encourage a strong emphasis on visibility and peer reviews within the team. (e.g. see pair programming in the *Software Reviews and Inspections* case study.) In this case, it is the team itself that is responsible for reviews. Of course, the project board or manager may also wish to initiate review activities at a broader level.

These questions of budget and ownership are intimately linked to governance and organizational adoption of reviews. We will come back to them in Parts III and IV.

OTHER OPTIONS

Reviews aren't a panacea. If projects begin to fail when they lose touch with reality, then it makes sense to do everything we can to shine a clear light onto what is going on within our projects. Project reviews are a complement to activities such as the following, not a replacement for them:

- Well-defined milestones (or inch pebbles), with clear acceptance criteria for each milestone: Thinking about the definition of success up front makes it harder to fool yourself when you get to the milestone.

- Frequent iterations with unambiguous deliverables: I remember a time when I was a technical architect and a project manager asked me whether an architecture document would be ready by the end of the week. I replied: 'I could deliver a document that looks great. You'd love it. The client would love it. It's only in six months time, when the team can't implement it, that you'll realize it's a pile of garbage. We need to address the following issues before we close the architecture... .' Look for deliverables that don't lie about their status. On software projects, this means working code.

- Clear metrics: Take time to think about ways you can meaningfully measure quality and progress.

- Information radiators: Use public charts and whiteboards to display status and progress, making it openly available to everyone. Besides needing the information to plan their own activities, people will use the openness as an opportunity to update, correct and clarify the information. If this dialogue isn't happening, then that also tells you something about the state of the project.

These activities all enhance the effectiveness of reviews. Having well-defined milestones with unambiguous deliverables and open displays of information means that reviewers can quickly assess status, then focus their energy on the areas that are murkier or riskier. Thus, they can maximize the value they add.

Finally, reviews do not replace the need for project managers and teams to manage their own projects. Review teams provide an independent perspective on status and issues, but it is project teams who have the day-to-day insight into what's going on, and who use this insight to deliver the project. Reviews are simply part of the support infrastructure for project teams, managers, sponsors and other stakeholders.

ASSURANCE OR AUDIT?

One final option to consider is audit. The difference between assurance and audit generates much debate in some quarters. Here is my take on their roles.

Audit assesses whether the project is operating in accordance with the relevant policies and standards, as defined by the organization, its regulators and other stakeholders. The definition of 'relevance' requires some judgement, but the underlying assumption is that the standards are correct and the auditors are primarily checking compliance with these standards. Because standards and policies are generally implemented through processes and controls, audit tends to focus on whether these processes and controls are operating as intended. Auditors typically report to stakeholders (often the CFO) who are not directly concerned with the project's success, but rather are interested in ensuring that the organization's assets are being used wisely.

Assurance focuses on whether the project is likely to succeed, and what can be done to help it succeed. In order to do this, it looks at processes and their alignment to good practice, but may also range more widely across other attributes of the project. It may be more forwards-looking than audit, focusing on what will happen ('Will the project succeed?') rather than what has happened ('Are the controls operating as intended?'). Assurance teams typically report to people with a more direct stake in the success of the project – project sponsors or portfolio managers.

Despite these differences, there are many similarities between audit and assurance. For a start, both need to be independent of the project team. Because they have this external perspective, they have more chance of seeing things that the project team is missing and are less likely to be caught up in the same misunderstandings (or fraudulent activities).

More fundamentally, in a healthy organization the policies and standards have been defined with a view to ensuring success. Thus, compliance with these standards is one way of improving the chances of success. (Again, it requires judgement as to whether this is the best way – generally applicable standards may require variation for specific circumstances.) So audit and assurance are really operating with the same end goal – trying to maximize the likelihood of success. They are just operating from slightly different perspectives as they do this.

So, there is a lot of overlap between audit and assurance. As a word, audit has negative connotations for many people. You need to be sensitive to this, as such perceptions can get in the way of an effective working relationship. Otherwise, I'd focus on the common goal to deliver projects and hence organizational objectives more effectively, and devote my energy to finding the best way to do this. One thing is clear here: it helps if audit and assurance teams work together to align their plans and share information, thus reducing duplication of effort for themselves and the project teams. (You may not be able to eliminate this duplication completely – auditors may have statutory and regulatory obligations that don't apply to review and assurance teams, and that require them to undertake some activities for themselves.)

THE CHALLENGES OF RUNNING EFFECTIVE REVIEWS

OK, so reviews are a good way to help projects keep in touch with reality. They can be tailored to a wide range of circumstances, from formal gateways to small, informal evaluations and self-assessments. Why is it that our projects are failing? Why are we not using reviews to catch problems early and hence to resolve them before they blow up?

Reviews are hard. As I speak with review teams, they identify a wide range of challenges that they face as they try to shine a light onto their projects. For example:

- It's hard to know who to talk to on the project team. There's never enough time to talk to everyone. You often only find out about some key person right towards the end of the review.

- It's hard to know what questions to ask. People come up with a wide range of issues and it's hard to know which to focus on. At the same time, there are often key things that they leave unsaid.

- It's hard to gather credible evidence. For example, some people will only talk 'off the record', yet their managers won't believe 'unattributed gossip'.

- It's easy to get overwhelmed by the amount of information. Projects can produce an enormous amount of documentation – which should you read and which can you ignore?

- It's easy to get confused. How do you sort out the truth from amongst the different, conflicting stories that people tell you? Particularly when you're not a technical specialist in the areas they're talking about?

- You can lose faith in your own judgement. People have said to me: 'Sometimes I feel like I'm going mad – I see clear issues with the project, yet no-one will believe me when I call them out.'

- Basic logistics can consume a lot of time. It's easy to underestimate the effort required to do things like accessing people's diaries, coordinating schedules and booking meeting rooms.

- Reviewers find it difficult to juggle conflicting demands, particularly when they are managing their own projects.

- Many people may see reviews as simply another layer of organizational bureaucracy. Reviews teams need to think about how they can demonstrate the value that they're delivering.

These difficulties generally fall into three broad areas:

1. Reviews always have limited time and resources. It can be challenging to agree terms of reference, get up to speed with a project, identify who to talk to, gather the appropriate information and then develop a final report within these constraints.

2. It can be difficult, and extremely frustrating, to get people to act on the findings from a review.

3. Organizational support for reviewers is often patchy. It's often difficult to persuade organizations to invest systematically in reviews. Review teams can become isolated, outside mainstream career paths and support structures.

The balance of this book looks at these three challenges in turn. Part II looks at the process of setting up and performing reviews. If reviewers have a clear model of the process they will undertake, they can focus their energy on defining objectives and gathering and analysing information. Without this clear model, time gets wasted simply thinking about what needs to be done next.

Part III looks at how reviews inform organizational decision making. If reviewers can create outputs that align closely to their audience's interests and scope of control, they maximize the likelihood that people will act on their findings. This section develops a simple model to help reviewers navigate these questions.

Finally, Part IV discusses some of the issues of embedding a review and assurance process within an organization.

CASE STUDY

Formal Gateways in the Public Sector

It's not clear exactly how much the UK public sector spends on projects: no central register is kept. However, we know it's a lot. The public sector procures £125 billion of goods and services per annum (NAO, 2006; HM Treasury, 2007). A significant percentage of that will be done through projects. Add in the cost of civil servants working on projects and it seems likely that the UK spends an eleven-figure sum on projects each year.

Exercising appropriate control on this spend is important. Accordingly, the Office of Government Commerce (OGC) has instigated a rigorous programme of gateway reviews for major projects. (OGC 2004b, OGC 2004c and OGC 2008)

WHAT IS AN OGC GATEWAY™ REVIEW?

A gateway is an independent review by an experienced team, conducted at a key decision point in a project or programme. It is intended to provide assurance to the Senior Responsible Owner (SRO – person accountable for success of the project or programme) that it is fit to proceed to the next stage.

WHICH PROJECTS UNDERGO GATEWAY REVIEWS?

The OGC oversaw 1500 gateway reviews on over 700 projects between 2001 and 2006. These include IT, construction and organizational change projects.

All substantial projects undergo reviews. The degree of rigour and resources applied to each review is determined by the risk level of the project – high-risk projects undergo substantial reviews by a team from outside the department performing the project; very low-risk projects undergo less formal reviews by internal reviewers. The risk level is determined by the SRO and programme manager, using a self-assessment template that considers factors such as the complexity of the project's drivers and stakeholders, the scale of the potential costs and benefits, the degree of innovation involved and the complexity of the contractual arrangements (e.g. OGC, 2004c). The overall aim is to allocate reviewing resources in proportion to the risk reduction that might be obtained from the review.

WHAT TYPE OF REVIEWS DO THESE PROJECTS UNDERGO?

Six types of gateway have been defined, aligned to different decision points in a project or programme:

1. Gate 0, Strategic Assessments, are scheduled at critical points in a programme (e.g. on completion of a tranche of projects). They aim to assess whether the programme remains aligned to organizational objectives, and whether it continues to be the best way to achieve these objectives. They ask questions such as:

    - Are the intended outcomes of the programme well defined, appropriate to the organization, and understood by all stakeholders?

    - Does the programme have clearly defined scope and success criteria?

    - Is the appropriate programme governance in place?

    - Have appropriate plans, project management, risk management, benefits realization and so on been established?

    - Are the necessary skills, finance and other resources available?

2. Gate 1, Business Justification, is conducted as each project is initiated. It aims to assure that the project's business case is well founded, and that the project is likely to deliver the expected outcomes. It considers factors such as the clarity of the business case; feasibility of delivering the objectives; and suitability of the implementation strategy, project structure and project management processes.

3. Gate 2, Delivery Strategy, is conducted prior to commencement of major procurements or implementations. It aims to assess the viability of the project approach and hence its suitability to progress to procurement or other major delivery activities. Considerations

include clarity and appropriateness of the specification, feasibility of the project plans and budgets, suitability of the chosen procurement strategy, and availability of the necessary funding, resources and skills.

4.   Gate 3, Investment Decision, is conducted prior to making major contractual and investment commitments. It confirms that procurement and supplier selection have undergone an appropriate process, and that the client and supplier together can implement the proposed solution and hence deliver the anticipated benefits. It also considers factors such as whether the business case continues to hold up, whether appropriate project management processes and controls are in place, and the suitability of the proposed solution and implementation plans.

5.   Gate 4, Readiness for Service, is conducted prior to deploying the solution. It confirms that the solution is ready for deployment and that the organization is ready to accept it. It considers factors such as completion of suitable quality assurance and acceptance testing, appropriateness of service introduction plans (including contingency and reversion plans), and the business case for wider deployment of the solution.

6.   Gate 5, Benefits Evaluation, is conducted after some period of operation of the solution in order to assess whether the anticipated benefits have been realized. It considers how well the solution or service has been operating, what benefits have been delivered, the suitability of any planned remedial actions or improvements to the service, and whether lessons learned from the project and operations have been captured and embedded within the organization.

Conducting these gateway reviews does not preclude the project or programme from conducting other reviews, for example interim design reviews or regular peer reviews, although such reviews would lie outside the gateway process. The OGC also stresses that gateway reviews are not audits.

HOW ARE THESE REVIEWS CONDUCTED?

The reviews are designed to be short, intense and focused. This minimizes the time during which the project team is disrupted, and ensures that the review delivers a clean snapshot of the project's status. The overall period from initiating the review to delivering the final report is typically eight to 12 weeks, with the review itself lasting three or four days.

The SRO and project manager are responsible for assessing the risk level of the project, and for contacting a central gateway review coordinator to schedule each review. (The self-assessment is repeated at each review point, in case the project's risk level has changed.) The coordinator works with them to confirm the risk assessment, manage timing and logistics of the review, and identify suitable reviewers. The review team typically has three or four members, depending on the risk level and complexity of the project. (For a low-risk project, a team of two people may be adequate.)

Once a review team has been identified, the project manager sends introductory project documentation to the team leader. About two to three weeks before the review, the team leader conducts a facilitated planning meeting with the review team and project leadership. This meeting clarifies the scope and objectives of the review, confirms the logistics and interview schedule, and identifies what project documentation is available. It may last a half or full day, depending on factors such as the size of the review and whether the teams have worked together before.

During the review itself, the first two to three days focus on gathering information through interviews and document reviews. On the final day, the review team finalizes their analysis, drafts a report, and presents it to the SRO. The final report is then delivered one to two weeks later. This report is typically short (six to 12 pages). Its objective is to convey key findings to the SRO and assign a RAG status to the project:

- Red: The project has issues that should be remedied as a matter of priority.
- Amber: The project has issues that should be remedied by the next gateway.
- Green: No major issues (although the review team may have made recommendations for improvement).

Finally, the central gateway team captures any examples of good practice or lessons learned that the review team identifies. These are then put into a generic form, for wider dissemination.

WHAT BENEFITS HAVE OGC GATEWAYS™

DELIVERED?

The Treasury estimates that, as of 2006, these reviews are delivering £1 billion of cost savings per annum. These savings come through reduced budget overruns and improved project outputs resulting from factors such as:

- ensuring that key stakeholders understand project status and are engaged at the appropriate points;

- confirming that project budgets, timescales and objectives are realistic;

- ensuring that the necessary skills are deployed on projects;

- giving the SRO assurance that the project is well founded, and hence allowing them to focus their attention on supporting the project manager and other stakeholders.

The reviews deliver an additional benefit in terms of building the skills of government staff through their participation in review teams.

WHAT CHALLENGES DO PEOPLE ENCOUNTER AS THEY CONDUCT REVIEWS?

OGC Gateways™ cover a wide range of projects and circumstances, so they can be expected to encounter a variety of challenges. Some of the most visible debates include:

- Confidentiality of findings: The final report from each review is delivered to the SRO and not published more widely. This helps ensure that the project team can discuss issues freely with the reviewers. On the other hand, it means that other stakeholders get no guaranteed visibility of issues identified by the review team.

- Acting on issues identified by reviews: The SRO is accountable for project success and hence for acting on the review team's findings as they see fit. Nonetheless, concerns have been raised that some major programmes have gone through multiple red gateways without addressing the issues identified by review teams. Reviewers have no way to escalate or enforce their findings in these circumstances. (The Treasury has recently established a Major Projects Review Group that may address this concern.)

- Lack of Gate 5 reviews: To date, relatively few gate 5 (Benefits Evaluation) reviews have been conducted, so it is still difficult to establish whether programmes are actually delivering the anticipated benefits. To some extent, this is a natural result of the time it takes for projects and programmes to get to this gateway.

In addition, the gateway process entails conducting a substantial number of reviews each year. Thus all the challenges of training and coordinating reviewers, managing logistics, and handling the intensity of reviews themselves will apply.

PART II
Project Review Process

There is never enough time. To conduct an effective review, we need to get up speed with a complex project, establish some sort of a relationship with key stakeholders and project team members, assimilate a wide range of dense and often conflicting information and hence integrate this all into a coherent set of findings that answers the original question posed by the review's sponsor. The last thing we need to do is spend a lot of time thinking about where to begin: anything that helps us hit the ground running is highly valuable.

This section develops a simple model for the review process. Its objective is to help understand what parameters drive a review and to explore the process of gathering and analysing information during the review. If these general attributes are clear to us, we can focus our energy on tailoring them to meet the objectives and on gathering the information relevant to this specific review for this particular project.

How can such a model help? I find that having a simple model of the key inputs, processes and outputs from a review, a model that I can carry around in my head, helps in a number of ways. For example:

- When someone stops me in the corridor to ask me what it would take to set up a review for project X, I can quickly identify the two or three questions I need to ask to establish the overall terms of reference for the review.

- When I'm working with a project manager to identify what documents I need to read and who I should interview during the review, the model helps me to narrow the possibilities down to a manageable subset.

- When an interviewee raises three or four issues in quick succession, I can think back to the review parameters and identify which issue I most need to follow up.

My goal isn't to set out a detailed, step-by-step process for conducting reviews. That doesn't help me when I'm on the spot in situations like the above. My goal is to describe something that can be contained in a single, simple diagram that I can remember.

Chapter 3 sets out this basic model. It couches a review as a system with inputs, outputs and feedback loops, and discusses how understanding these elements helps to plan and conduct a review.

Chapter 4 then examines the inputs and feedback loops in more detail.

One of these feedback loops links reviews to organizational learning – by capturing the lessons learned during reviews and retaining them in our bag of 'reference models' for future reviews, we begin to build learning into our review process. Chapter 5 explores this linkage between reviews and broader organizational learning.

Chapter 6 zooms back into the details of conducting a review. It examines the process of gathering and analysing information and discusses some key information gathering techniques.

As the saying goes in military circles: 'Amateurs talk tactics. Professionals talk logistics.' Basic logistics such as scheduling meetings and finding rooms can consume a lot of time if we're not careful. Chapter 7 discusses some of the things we need to think about here. If we can set these things up to run smoothly, we can focus our energy on higher value activities.

The Review Process

This chapter sets out a simple systems model for reviewing. The basic model has been derived from my experience with software quality assurance and reviewing (see, for example, Gilb and Graham, 1993; Weigers, 2002), but it's general enough to apply to most types of review. More importantly, it's simple enough for me to remember, so I can use it when I'm under pressure while working on a project or other review.

CONVENTIONAL MODEL

The first project review I participated in was very friendly. Half a dozen of us sat down in a meeting room and looked at each other. We smiled and introduced ourselves. The project manager explained the objectives and structure of the project. We discussed how things were going. We asked questions about risks. The reviewers put forward random suggestions designed as much to show how smart they were as to actually help the project. We told a few war stories, had a laugh and broke up.

I've since sat in an embarrassing number of reviews like that. Sometimes one of the random suggestions hits the mark and the project team takes away an idea that will actually help their project. Sometimes we all felt better after having a grumble about our project sponsors. That boost to morale must be worth something? Mostly, however, these reviews were a waste of time.

In more organized environments, we had detailed checklists to work from. These covered questions in areas such as:

- Is there a clear business case for the project? Are the assumptions behind that business case still valid?

- Are the project plans, solution designs and other work elements defined? Are they stable? Do they deliver the capabilities called for by the business case?

- Is the project progressing as expected? Have the anticipated tasks been completed? Have the expected deliverables been delivered to an appropriate level of quality?

- Have key risks been identified, and are they being actively managed?

- Are the necessary control processes (change management, financial and budgetary control, escalation, and so on) in place and functioning effectively?

These checklists were very handy. They were also very long. In practice, this meant we were trying to cover a lot of ground very quickly. We ended up with a lot of ticks on the checklists, and little real understanding of the project. We would almost certainly have added much more value if we'd picked one aspect of the checklist – say the business case, or the quality of the deliverables – and focused our energy on gaining some insight into it. The question was: which aspect should we focus on?

These checklists also led to a lot of debate. Project managers often had strong opinions as to why elements of the organization's standard processes didn't apply to their project. Technologists were prepared to argue endlessly about what constitutes good design. On some reviews, we spent more time debating abstract notions of what constitutes 'best practice' than we spent looking at what the project was actually doing. If our primary role was to help this project keep in touch with reality, then we failed.

THE SYSTEMS MODEL

These experiences have persuaded me that effective project reviews need more structure than a simple meeting or checklist. To add most value, reviewers need to be able to do four things:

- They need to agree terms of reference with the review's sponsor. In particular, they need to agree where they should focus their energy. Without focus, effort gets diffused across a wide range of topics and the review may never drill deeply enough into any single topic to add value.

- They need to identify where they will look for information – what documents they will read, who they will interview, what other data might be relevant. Without clear focus, defined in the terms of reference, this easily becomes overwhelming.

- They need to be able to identify what standards and 'good practices' they will review against. Without a solid foundation here, reviews waste effort on abstract discussions of project management theory.

- They need a clear understanding of what activities they will undertake and how these relate to the overall objectives for the review. This enables them to plan their time, focusing it on gathering and analysing information that helps achieve their objectives.

Figure 3.1 shows the model I use to help myself think about these four things.

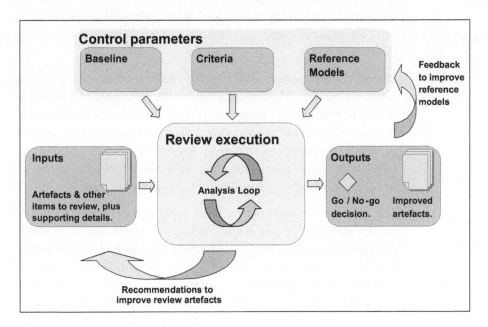

Figure 3.1   Systems model for a review

This model couches a review as a simple system with a number of inputs (e.g. interviews and documents) which it will transform into outputs (decisions, improved processes, and so on). It uses a variety of control parameters to determine how it makes this transformation, and a couple of feedback loops to help it inform wider processes. In terms of the above four needs, this model reminds me to think about:

- Terms of reference: These are determined by the outputs and the criteria. What outputs does this review inform – is it providing information for a particular investment decision, for example, or is it identifying ways to improve a specific aspect of the project? Which criteria will determine the quality of these outputs? If our decision to proceed with the project will be influenced primarily by its alignment to organizational objectives, let's focus our attention here rather than on basic project management practices. Conversely, if we're primarily concerned about whether a junior project manager has set up the project appropriately, we will focus on project management practices and processes.

- Information gathering: This is about inputs. What documents, interviews and other information do we need to look at? How can we access this information? How much detail do we need to go into? These are all important parameters for scoping and resourcing the review.

- Standards: These are divided into two elements: the baseline and the reference models. The baseline defines the elements of the project that have been agreed prior to this review and hence don't need to be challenged. If we're reviewing a plan, we measure it against the objectives it's supposed to deliver. If we're reviewing a design, we measure it against the specification. Without an agreed baseline, we have no clear way to determine if the project is on course.

  The reference models define what we'll accept as good practice for the purposes of this review. Whereas the baseline is probably relevant only to this project, reference models have wider utility. They may, for example, be defined by organizational policy or generally accepted practices within an industry. Thus, when reviewing a plan, we might measure it against the organization's standards for creating work breakdown structures. By agreeing these standards before we start the review, we can avoid unnecessary debates during its execution.

- Activities: The analysis loop (within the 'Review execution' box in Figure 3.1) defines the activities we need to undertake in order to gather and analyse information. Chapter 6 discusses this loop in more detail – it provides some models and heuristics for how review teams gather, record and analyse information. Understanding these activities helps reviewers to plan the review, and to hit the ground running when they start to engage with the project team.

The review feeds information back into the project and its stakeholders through the lower feedback loop ('Recommendations to improve review artefacts') in Figure 3.1, making recommendations as to how elements of the project or its environment could be modified to increase the likelihood of success.

The second feedback loop ('Feedback to improve reference models') is about organizational learning. As the review team identifies examples of good (or poor) practice in the course of each review, it records these into its reference models. These models then become a type of organizational memory: review teams use them to propagate good ideas and practices to other projects in the course of their reviews. Chapter 5 comes back to this role of reviews to support organizational learning.

Chapter 4 looks at all of these parameters in more detail. It's a simple model, but one where I can quickly run through the boxes in my mind whenever I'm setting up a review. Before we do this, I want to look more closely at what we need to think about as we initiate a review.

INITIATING A REVIEW – REVIEWS AS PROJECTS

Much of the above discussion sounds like basic project management: clarifying objectives; agreeing scope; working to an agreed methodology. That gives us another way to think about reviews – whether we're conducting a meeting that lasts two hours or a detailed health check that lasts two weeks, each review is just a small project. Figure 3.1 gives a simple model for planning and performing this project. So let's think about some of the key things we do as we set up such a project – chartering, scoping, roles and responsibilities, and communications.

CHARTERING – WHAT DO WE WANT TO ACHIEVE?

Here are some of the areas we need to agree with the sponsor as we're setting up a review:

- Who is the sponsor? This may be the project's sponsor, or it may be another person or body. If the review doesn't have a clear sponsor, it is likely to lack focus. It will also lack a clear path to escalate any issues it comes across (either with the project itself, or in conducting the review).

- Why are we conducting the review? We may be providing information to inform a particular decision or to clarify a particular aspect of the project. This will influence the type of information we need to gather and the depth of analysis we need to undertake. (In terms of Figure 3.1, what outputs are we creating and what criteria are we using?)

- Does the sponsor have any specific concerns? Sponsors often initiate reviews because there are aspects of the project that are troubling them. Knowing about this means that we can focus on clarifying these areas of the project. (These concerns will start out as hypotheses in our analysis loop – see Chapter 6.)

- Who else will we be reporting to? The way we couch our findings will be influenced by the audience – project team members need a different level of detail to senior executives, for example. A report that's confidential to the project sponsor may cover concerns that couldn't be expressed (or would need to be expressed differently) in an openly published document. Where a project spans multiple organizations (as when a consortium of contractors is working for a client), issues of confidentiality may be especially pertinent.

- In what format should we deliver our results? For an informal checkpoint, the output may be a simple list of agreed actions and owners. For a more substantial assessment, we may deliver a presentation backed by a detailed report. If we need to deliver a report, we need to plan time to write and review it.

- How detailed do these results need to be? People need sufficient information in order to act, without being overwhelmed by details. The dividing line varies widely, depending on the person receiving the information, the state of the project and the credibility of the review team. Sometimes we just need to make recommendations and they will be acted upon. Sometimes we need to build a detailed evidential chain connecting what we've seen and heard to root causes and hence to proposed actions. This takes a lot more work.

- When do we need to deliver the results?

- How should our interpretations be checked before we finalize our findings? It's common to check facts with interviewees, to confirm we've heard correctly. If we are also going to check our interpretations with them, we need to build in time to do it. Likewise, sometimes we will give project teams time to act on our findings before we report them more widely (see the *Earthquakes in the Project Portfolio* case study, for example). If an issue is fixed quickly, perhaps it doesn't need to go into our report at all? (Even so, we may want to retain it in our database, so we can analyse the frequency of its occurrence across projects and hence initiate process improvements if necessary.) All these protocols need to be agreed with our sponsor, so they know what information they're going to receive and when.

- Are there other reporting protocols that apply? Questions of confidentiality and attribution (do we attribute comments to specific interviewees, or are they anonymized?) often come up. Comments are much more credible if they are attributed, but people may feel safer to say some things 'off the record'. (The fact that this is the case is information in itself.) Likewise, there may be organizational or regulatory information management requirements about retention of notes and findings.

- What are the boundaries of the review? There may be aspects of the project that our sponsor doesn't want us to examine. Likewise, we need to agree what constitutes our baseline and reference models.

- Are there any preferences or constraints as to how we should run the review?

- What resources does the sponsor wish to invest in the review?

- What authority does the review team have, and what escalation paths should it use? The review team may have authority to go anywhere and talk to anyone (see the case study *Completion Bonds in the Film Industry*), or access might be entirely at the project manager's discretion. Likewise, the first point for escalation of issues may be the review sponsor, the project sponsor, or someone else.

- Are there any sensitivities we should be aware of, or other risks we might need to manage in the course of the review? Reviews often run into a range of sensitivities across the various stakeholders – it helps to know about them, and to plan how to deal with them. Likewise, as with any project, it's worth considering whether there are other risks that might jeopardize effective completion of the review and acceptance of its findings.

These questions are mostly about clarifying the outputs from the review: what they are and why they're needed. For any substantial review, I'd want to agree written terms of reference with the sponsor before I commence. The act of going through these questions (or those of them that apply: some may be predetermined by organizational policy, for example) and writing down the answers helps me be clear about what I need to do.

SCOPING – WHO SHOULD WE TALK TO?

Once we know what we're aiming to deliver, the next question is generally: what information do we need to gather? For most reviews, this leads quickly to: who do we need to talk to? There are several dimensions to consider when planning interview coverage:

- Role: It's useful to get perspectives from a range of roles on the project. Differences in viewpoint between the sponsor, project manager and team members can be very instructive. Likewise, people with different functions (graphic designers versus engineers, for example) may have quite different perspectives.

- Organization: If the project involves people from multiple organizations (client, supplier, perhaps other stakeholders such as regulators), it's worth understanding their different drivers and perceptions.

- Team: If the project is structured into a number of teams, even if they have similar functions (say multiple construction teams), it may be worth gathering perspectives from different teams. As well as formal teams, people may have organized themselves into informal groups – these can be harder to track down, but it can be worthwhile to sample across such teams also.

- Time and place: If the project is dispersed across multiple locations or is working multiple shifts, this can be another interesting source of differing views and perceptions.

- Experience: It can be worthwhile talking both to people who have recently joined the organization or project, and to people who have been around for a long time. New joiners may see things that everyone else has become inured to. Old hands understand the history and the underlying tensions that new people may not yet be attuned to. People who have recently been promoted or otherwise changed role may have useful insights too.

- Changes: People who have left the project are often another source of useful information. Again, they may understand aspects of the history that people on the project don't. They may also feel less inhibited to raise some subjects.

- Personality: This is another dimension that can be difficult to track down, but sampling across a range of personalities (e.g. extrovert versus introvert, reflective versus active, pessimistic versus optimistic) may reveal a range of interesting perceptions.

- Politics: Sometimes we need to speak to people simply to manage the political sensitivities around the project. If we speak to the head of one department, the head of another department may feel slighted if we don't also talk to them. If we don't interview one manager, then they'll feel that their views aren't represented and won't accept our findings. It can be difficult to map out all these sensitivities, and if the review's sponsor is sufficiently powerful, or the findings are sufficiently clear, we may be able to bypass them. On the other hand, it can be much easier to gain support for our findings if we manage these politics from the outset. This can be particularly important if we're running an ongoing programme of reviews.

That sounds like a lot of interviews. In practice, the first six or 12 interviews often raise most of the substantive issues. After that, we're mostly filling in details, gathering confirmatory evidence and handling some of the political sensitivities. (Don't underestimate the latter: it may not affect your findings, but it will almost certainly affect whether people accept and act on your findings.) If significant new issues are coming to our attention after a dozen or more interviews, then that itself says something about the coherence of the project team and effectiveness of its internal communications.

Of course, the Terms of Reference will drive the exact selection of interviewees, perhaps leading us to focus on certain roles or teams. Nonetheless, our initial aim would generally be to gather a range of viewpoints as quickly as possible. We may then want to explore or verify some of these viewpoints during our later interviews. It is a good idea for the initial interview plan to leave some slots open towards the end of the information gathering phase for this exploration. These slots can be used either to revisit interviewees for clarification, or to include additional people who can shed light on specific issues.

This exploration and verification is especially important when issues are contentious. Where people have highly divergent opinions or there are strong divisions across the project team and other stakeholders, these latter interviews can help us gather sufficient evidence to build a clear perspective on the situation. This is also the case when individuals raise strong concerns that aren't widely shared. Joe may be a pessimist, but he may also be seeing something that others are missing: we need to identify which is the case.

BUILDING THE REVIEW TEAM – ROLES AND RESPONSIBILITIES

The review team itself needs to include, or have access to, people in four broad roles:

- Review team leader: The leader works with the review's sponsor to set the terms of reference. They then identify the skills needed and recruit the other team members, initiate planning for the review and establish contact (either directly or via the review sponsor) with the project team. They carry overall responsibility for the review's findings and recommendations, assuring that they are well framed (e.g. that the findings are backed by appropriate evidence, and that the recommendations address the main issues) and presented in a form that can be understood by the people receiving them.

- Review team member: Review team members gather and analyse information during the course of the review. Ideally, they will be trained in techniques for interviewing, information analysis, and so on. They may also bring specialist expertise to the team, for example in a technical discipline or project management specialism. Chapter 11 discusses the skills profile for review team members in more detail.

  Some organizations include a mix of experienced reviewers and more junior people on their review teams (e.g., see the *Assuring Fixed Price Implementations* case study). This can be a good way for people to learn review skills and see a wider range of projects, thus growing personal skills and organizational capability.

- Specialist skills: Depending on the project and the review's objectives, a review team may need to call on a wide range of specialist expertise. This may include expertise in specific technologies or business functions, project management and procurement disciplines, legal or financial skills, specialist audit or assurance techniques, and so on. Such experts might either be part of the review team, or made available to them for consultation as necessary. Alternatively, it may be worthwhile to set up preparatory or supplementary reviews, for example contract reviews by legal and commercial specialists or design and architecture reviews by technical specialists.

- Administrative support: Tasks such as scheduling meetings, arranging meeting rooms, archiving files and disseminating reports can take a surprising amount of effort. Good administrative support allows reviewers to focus on gathering and analysing information. (Chapter 7 discusses these logistical issues in more detail.)

COMMUNICATIONS – ESTABLISHING CONTACT WITH THE PROJECT TEAM

It is worth making contact with the project team at an early stage. Even if the review team has authority to go wherever it pleases and speak to whomever it wants, it's generally much easier to conduct an effective review when there is a good working relationship. Thus, it's a good idea to schedule a preliminary meeting with the project's leadership team. Table 7.2 (page 160) sets out a possible agenda for this meeting. (Chapter 7 discusses communication with the project team in more detail. See also the case study *Formal Gateways in the Public Sector*, and the discussion on interview preparation in Chapter 6.)

CASE STUDY

Lesson from Problems in the Past

Pioneer Natural Resources is a fast growing Fortune 1000 oil and gas exploration company based in Dallas, Texas. It creates value through a combination of successful drilling, efficient development of its reserves and cost-conscious operations.

WHAT IS THE SIZE AND SHAPE OF YOUR PROJECT PORTFOLIO?

A significant proportion of our $30M IT budget goes into project work. We are a 'buy not build' shop, so many of our projects are about application selection, integration and implementation. We have a lean staff and an aging workforce. (like everyone else in the oil and gas industry)

WHAT SORT OF REVIEWS DO YOU PERFORM?

Peer reviews are required on all high-profile projects, for example those with a large budget, high risk, high visibility or a high level of integration. For such projects, we'll do at least one and sometimes two reviews. Reviews of low-profile projects are optional.

HOW DO YOU CONDUCT THESE REVIEWS?

The PMO (Project Management Office) and department head assign the review team. This might contain from seven to 20 people with a broad range of skills – IT upper management, data, networking, infrastructure and more.

The team formally covers the review in one or two sessions that last about an hour each. Outside of these formal meetings, other meetings and activities occur depending on the scope and timing of the project.

We capture the results of the review into a standard template. However, the real value is associated with the questions and the dialogue at the reviews more than the actual documented results. The reviews are for our own department, so we don't need to report them more widely.

WHAT VALUE DO THE REVIEWS ADD?

They make people think beyond their preferences and specific client requests to consider the overall impact to our organization. They also promote discussion around key areas where we have had problems in the past – infrastructure, data management, planning, testing challenges. For example, how and where do we benchmark performance in remote locations such as an island in Alaska or a rig in Nigeria? Sometimes we focus on the risks we need to manage.

WHAT CHALLENGES DO REVIEW TEAMS RUN INTO?

We're better at identifying small tactical things that can be addressed easily (e.g. 'we need to check with the guys in Tunisia to see if they can access this'). It can be hard to get up to speed with the project context, business drivers and other factors fast enough to ask strategic questions. People also may not challenge the approach or anything that could impact timelines and budgets because they don't want people to do it to one of their projects. Sometimes people are passive aggressive and take their feedback outside of the meeting through less effective routes.

We are working on building an environment that can handle healthy debates better. We're also working on getting reviews scheduled earlier in the planning process, to avoid people simply wanting everyone to sign off their plan.

WHAT CHALLENGES HAVE YOU RUN INTO IN SETTING UP THE REVIEW PROCESS?

We were a self-described 'ready-fire-aim' department with silos and operating at CMM[1] level 1 a few years ago. (We're slightly above level 2 at this point.) Many of the people who were successful in that environment saw this as time-consuming fluff or 'administrivia'. These people are confident that they

---

1   Capability Maturity Model, see Humphrey, 1989.

know best, but are willing to go through the exercise because it is mandatory. Sometimes it comes across as something they just need to check off their list.

Newer and less experienced people may find the most value in the reviews, but it's tricky for them too: they are cautious not to spend too much time on the feedback or to appear that they don't already have all the answers.

WHAT PLANS DO YOU HAVE FOR REVIEWS IN THE FUTURE?

We do not have independent assessments at this point, but it is being discussed. The CIO (Chief Information Officer) has stated that he supports this approach. I think independent assessments will promote discussion of the more strategic questions, and help build an environment for cross-department feedback.

ACKNOWLEDGEMENTS

With thanks to Lynn Lyon, Pioneer Natural Resources.

Review Parameters

Chapter 3 introduced a simple model to help think about the way we set up reviews. This chapter discusses the parameters of that model in more detail, and looks at their influence on the way we conduct reviews. It then explores how these parameters vary across the project lifecycle, informing the type of review that we might conduct at any given point.

OUTPUTS

We undertake reviews in order to achieve some outcome, so it is useful to start with outputs – the information that the review is intended to produce. Reviews typically produce two types of output:

- Information to inform a decision about the project: This may be a decision as to whether to continue investment in the project, for example a gate review that informs a go/no-go decision. It may be a decision about when to announce a new product, or about whether to initiate contingency actions on a dependent project. This information is primarily intended to help stakeholders outside the project team.

- Information to inform the way we run the project: This may be recommendations to improve project management processes, or identification of risks that need to be managed, or escalation of issues that need attention by the sponsor, and so on. This information is intended primarily for people within the project team.

As the saying goes, no-one can serve two masters. Reviews that try to support both internal and external stakeholders risk serving neither well. As we set up reviews, therefore, it pays to identify which stakeholders represent our primary audience and what information they need to inform their decisions and actions. This then determines the type of information we gather, the way we analyse it and the way we present our findings. (Of course, much of the information we produce may turn out to be useful to both sets of stakeholders. That shouldn't prevent us focusing on our primary audience. Being clear about this primary audience doesn't just help us focus our energy: it also helps us manage the expectations of other people we talk to during the course of the review.)

Reviews may also produce other outputs. They may, for example, trigger escalation processes if they come across certain types of information. Evidence of fraud or criminal activity is the obvious (although, fortunately, uncommon) escalation point – if we uncover such evidence, we need to notify the appropriate authorities. Likewise, if we find evidence of substantial problems with a project, we may need to escalate outside the 'standard' reporting lines. Again, it helps to be clear up front about what sort of issues we will need to escalate, and how we will escalate them, both for our own effectiveness and for the sake of managing expectations.

Finally, the visibility into project status and operations that reviews provide may help instil confidence that the project portfolio is under control. This may be less tangible than the other outputs, but if it helps the organization to address additional opportunities, then it's an invaluable outcome.

CONTROL PARAMETERS

Chism (2007) notes that three things are at the heart of an effective peer review process: criteria, evidence and standards. Criteria and standards appear in the systems model as control parameters. Standards are subdivided into baseline (that which is agreed for this project prior to the review) and reference models (which are agreed more widely, for example by organizational policy). Together, these define the reference points against which we will review the project. Criteria then define how we will assess whether the project remains aligned to these standards. We will come to evidence gathering in Chapter 6.

BASELINE

The baseline defines those parts of the project that have been agreed prior to the review. The baseline may be axiomatic or it may have been covered by earlier reviews. For example, the organization's business strategy is typically axiomatic: we don't question it during a project review, but rather we review the project's business case to confirm it's aligned to the overall strategy. Likewise, once the business case has been reviewed and approved, subsequent reviews don't need to re-examine it in detail: they can focus on questions such as whether the project plans can feasibly deliver the objectives it defines.

These examples illustrate how we use the baseline as a point of reference: we review the current state of the project to confirm it's consistent with ('aligned to', 'can feasibly deliver') the baseline. We can't necessarily ignore the baseline completely as we do this (in the above example, we may want confirm that any assumptions contained in the business case still hold at subsequent reviews), but understanding our baseline helps us focus our energy elsewhere.

REFERENCE MODELS

Reference models contain the body of standards, policies, commonly agreed practices, and so on, that apply to projects of this type in this organization. For a construction project, they might include elements such as building regulations, planning guidelines and organizational procurement policies. For a software engineering project, they may include architectural principles, coding standards, user interface design guidelines, security policies, lifecycle models, and so on.

We typically review the project to assess whether it conforms to these reference models. This can engender a lot of debate. Often we have multiple, overlapping standards to choose from: people will have different opinions as to which ones apply. Likewise, every project is different and people will have opinions as to how the general standards need to be varied to suit the circumstances of this specific project.

These debates eat time. It generally doesn't help to get caught up in them. The best way I know to maintain focus during the review is to agree up front which reference models apply for this project, and how and why they have been varied. This is done either when setting the initial terms of reference with the review sponsor, or when having the initial meeting with the project leadership. A project that can't agree its reference models probably has other communication problems to contend with too, so failure to agree on reference models is itself useful information for reviewers. (Audits, by the way, generally don't have this problem – the auditors get to define which reference models they're going to assess the project against.)

Reviewers also have their own toolkit of reference models. We use checklists to capture useful practices for reviews – useful questions to ask, or common problems that occur on projects in our organization, or such like. These are a type of reference model. Chapter 5 discusses how we can use these reference models as an element of organizational memory, capturing common issues and good practices that we can disseminate to other projects through the review process.

CRITERIA

The baseline and reference models can represent a large body of information in themselves. Trying to assess a project against every applicable standard, for example, would probably take longer than the project. Criteria tell us which elements of the baseline and which reference models we want to assess the project against, and how we want to make that assessment. For example:

- The review may focus on assessing the project's progress against the baseline schedule and budget.

- It may focus on assessing whether the project's outputs remain aligned to the objectives contained in the baseline business case.

- We may be more interested in whether particular project management processes and controls are consistent with 'best practice'. In this case, we're probably not interested in every possible process – trying to evaluate a project against the entire PMBOK is pretty well intractable. In thinking about our criteria, we're making a judgement as to which are most likely to be important for this project. If it's building a complex system for a rapidly changing environment, we may be most interested in configuration management and change control, for example.

- Or we may be interested primarily in whether deliverables are likely to meet applicable quality standards. Again, we probably can't assess against every possible standard, rather we choose which ones are most important to this phase of the project.

The number of possibilities is endless. The important thing is that we think about where we want to focus up front, so that we can plan our resources appropriately and manage expectations with our stakeholders. My experience is that reviews add most value when they focus on no more than two or three criteria. Beyond that, they start to skate across the surface, never gathering sufficient depth of information to create actionable findings in any area.

Where does this leave us when someone asks us to 'just do a general review of the project'? As I noted earlier, this can generally be reframed to focus on two criteria: are the objectives well defined and understood, and are the primary risks to those objectives being managed appropriately? In other words:

- Our baseline is the organization's business strategy and the business case for the project. Our review aims to confirm that the business case identifies clear objectives, and that these objectives are driving stakeholder actions.

- Our reference models focus on risk management processes and associated tools (such as checklists). Our review aims to check that these are being used effectively on the project.

In the course of our initial interviews, we may uncover risks that aren't being managed. In that case, we might choose to initiate another iteration of reviewing to drill down into the most threatening risks. The criteria for these latter reviews would then be tailored to each specific risk.

This example also illustrates how we can cover more than two or three criteria: break the problem down into several reviews, or several iterations within a single review, each of which focuses on a small number of criteria. This pattern of an initial broad-ranging review with follow-up activities to drill into specific risks is common. An alternative pattern of deep reviews to assure the quality of specific deliverables followed by a broad review to assess the overall progress and status of the project is also common.

As well as agreeing the criteria and their associated reference models and baseline, it is worthwhile thinking about the degree of rigour with which we will apply the criteria. For example, what tolerances can we live with when deciding if delays or budget overruns are material to our assessment? Do we expect the project to comply rigidly with a standard, or is there latitude for variation? How much latitude? Tightly defined standards generally make the review easier: it will be easier to come to an objective assessment of whether the standards are being met. However, if the project is trying to do something innovative, it may need more latitude to adapt its approach as it learns. We need to adapt our review approach accordingly.

In the wider context, if reviewers get a reputation for rigidly applying standards without adaptation to specific project circumstances, they are likely to experience resistance from project managers and teams. Conversely, reviewers who are seen to be helpful in tailoring standards to match the project's situation will be welcomed as useful advisers. This opens up lines of communication and makes it much easier to conduct effective reviews.

INPUTS

Once we've established what we're trying to achieve and our overall approach, we can start to identify the specific inputs we'll need. Inputs may include:

- Documents and supporting materials: These are especially useful for preliminary reading to understand the project and develop an interview protocol.

- Interviews: These are often our main tool for probing and understanding what is actually happening on the project.

- Status reports, risk registers, self-assessment checklists and associated artefacts: These are all useful for telling us about the perceived current state of the project.

- Workshops: As an alternative or supplement to interviews, workshops can be a good way to gather and analyse information.

- Prototypes and other examples: A good way to get a handle on project outputs and deliverables.

- Observation: You can learn a lot about what is happening on a project simply by observing how people are working, their communication patterns, the ad hoc meetings they are calling to address issues, and so on.

The bulk of our planning will revolve around identifying which mix of these inputs we need to assess the project against the agreed criteria. Understanding the criteria helps us narrow down the inputs to a manageable subset. (This is often an iterative process: the inputs available to us may influence what we can realistically achieve.)

REVIEW EXECUTION – THE ANALYSIS LOOP

The main phase of the review is about gathering and analysing information. This can be framed as a process of generating hypotheses and then gathering the information needed to confirm or refute them (e.g. see the case study *Review Techniques in the Education Sector*).

Our criteria drive the initial set of hypotheses that we will investigate. For example, where we are assessing the project's progress against the baseline schedule and budget, we might start with the hypothesis that the project is on schedule and then look for evidence to suggest that it isn't. Chapter 6 discusses this process in more detail.

Factors such as the following will also influence the way in which we plan and execute this analysis loop:

- Are there any constraints on our access to the project team and documentation? Geographically distributed teams or tight security requirements, for example, can have a substantial impact on scheduling. Even simple logistical details such as availability of meeting rooms can have a strong influence on our plans.

- Is this a one-off review or health check, or is it part of an ongoing programme of reviews or assurance? In the latter case, outputs from earlier reviews may influence our investigations, for example, to check that issues identified during those reviews have been addressed.

- Will we need specialist expertise for certain parts of the review and, if so, how will we coordinate with the relevant experts?

- Will we hold intermediate checkpoints with the review sponsor and/ or project manager? These are a useful way to confirm that we are covering the right territory and are making reasonable interpretations of the information we're gathering. However, we need both to schedule time for them, and to schedule preparation time to analyse and structure our findings so that we can make best use of them.

It's easy to underestimate the amount of time that needs to be invested in analysis, report writing and communicating with stakeholders. My rule of thumb is that every hour of interviewing generates about two hours of analysis and other activities. (That means, for example, that 12 one-hour interviews imply a total effort of 36 hours, or three intense days during the main phase of the review plus additional time to write the final report. Every time I try to cut corners, perhaps reducing my time to analyse interview notes in order to schedule additional interviews, I end up regretting it.)

FEEDBACK LOOPS

Figure 3.1 (page 57) shows two feedback loops. The first of these, 'Recommendations to improve project', is the standard loop whereby the review team delivers recommendations to the project team and other stakeholders.

The second loop, 'Feedback to improve reference models' is the organizational learning loop that we will discuss in Chapter 5. Given that the reference models effectively constitute our organization's memory of good practices, this feedback can be especially powerful: when reviewers improve and disseminate these models, they can affect a wide range of projects.

REVISITING REVIEW TYPES

Chapter 2 discussed the different types of review we can undertake. This section revisits that discussion to explore how the above parameters interact with the type of review.

TIMING OF REVIEWS

As we move through the project lifecycle, we review and agree additional elements of the project – plans, specifications, designs, and so on. Thus successive reviews build from the baseline established by earlier reviews. Table 4.1 illustrates the series of event-based reviews that this might lead to. (This is only illustrative: the specific sequence of reviews will be tailored to an organization's lifecycle, policies and business strategy. The gates described in the *Formal Gateways in the Public Sector* case study illustrate another sequence of reviews.) Reviewers might also use a subset of a checklist such as that in Table 5.2 (pages 100–117) to guide these reviews, choosing the questions relevant to each stage of the project.

In the phase between the Architecture and Release gate reviews in Table 4.1, the organization might then conduct periodic status and risk reviews. These would use the project plan as a baseline, gathering evidence such as completion of milestones and deliverables to assess whether progress is consistent with this baseline. (Separate quality reviews of the deliverables might also inform these assessments.) Likewise, they might aim to assess whether the project's risk identification and management processes are operating effectively, as evidenced by a complete and actively maintained risk register. (Of the case studies, both *Earthquakes in the Project Portfolio* and *Assuring Fixed Price Implementation* used approaches similar to this.)

If concerns arise about the project or about changes in the external environment at any point, the organization might also initiate one-off health checks. The parameters for these would be tailored to the specific circumstances.

Table 4.1 A sequence of event-based gate reviews

Review	Objectives	Baseline	Reference models	Criteria
Business case	Confirm business case is viable and aligned to overall strategy	Organizational strategy	Standards for return on investment (ROI) calculations and sensitivity analysis	ROI appropriately calculated and above hurdle rate; Alignment to overall strategy
Project definition	Confirm project can deliver the agreed business case	Business case	Project planning guidelines; Risk management guidelines	Alignment to business case Conformance to planning guidelines; Completeness of risk analysis
Specification	Confirm systems can deliver project objectives	Business case	Systems specification guidelines and standards	Consistency with objectives in business case; Conformance to guidelines
Architecture	Confirm systems can deliver project objectives	Specification	Enterprise architecture	Consistency with specification; Alignment to enterprise architecture principles
Release	Confirm systems can be safely released into operations	Specification Business case	Operations manual	Consistency with specification; Continued viability of business case; Conformance to operations principles and standards

DEGREE OF INDEPENDENCE AND FORMALITY

These are largely independent of the parameters in Figure 3.1 (page 57) they are set more by the degree of assurance required and the amount that we are prepared to invest to obtain it.

ATTRIBUTES BEING REVIEWED

Table 4.2 illustrates baseline and reference models that might apply when reviewing the project attributes discussed in Chapter 2. (Again, this is only an illustrative list. Every organization will build its own list of assets and standards over time.)

Table 4.2　　Examples of standards applying to different attributes of the project

Attribute	Baseline	Reference models
Objectives	• Organizational strategy • Business case	• Methods such as sensitivity and options analysis
Status	• Project plan, schedule and budgets • Earlier status reports	• Organizational standards for status tracking and reporting • Standard techniques and metrics such as Earned Value
Risk	• Business case • Project plan • Earlier versions of risk register	• Organizational standards for risk management • Standard approaches and models for risk management • Management of Risk (M_o_R; OGC, 2002) • Checklists of lessons learned from earlier projects
Quality	• Quality plan • Specifications • Test plans	• Relevant ISO, IEEE and other standards • Relevant regulations and legislation • Organizational policies, standards and guidelines
Process	• Project plan	• Bodies of knowledge such as APM (2006) and Project Management Institute (PMI) (2004) • Methodologies and approaches such as PRINCE2, MSP, M_o_R
Compliance		• Relevant quality or process standards and policies from above lists • Organizational policies and standards • Relevant regulations and legislation

ASSURANCE OR AUDIT?

The separation between baseline and reference models also helps clarify the distinction between assurance and audit. We noted in the Chapter 2 that audit focuses on compliance with policies and standards. Thus, as a rough and ready rule, we might expect auditors to focus on assessing the project against reference models. Assurance teams are likely to give more weight to the baseline – is the project still doing what it set out to do, and is that still worth doing? (This is by no means absolute: the two functions will be interested in both types of standard. They simply have a different overall focus.)

CASE STUDY

Post-project Reviews and Retrospectives

Many organizations have trouble with post-project reviews. We all know they're a good idea, but once the project is winding down and the team is dispersing, it can be difficult to find energy for a review. If the review does happen, it's often little more than an unstructured discussion about people's gripes. If any useful ideas do come up, it's hard to get anyone else to pay attention to them. Knowing this, no-one makes attending post-project reviews a priority, and the cycle continues.

Fortunately, agile software development approaches have reinvigorated the idea of conducting learning-oriented reviews at the end of iterations, phases and projects. Some good books (Kaner *et al.*, 1996; Kerth, 2001; Derby and Larsen, 2006) have assembled a range of techniques for planning and conducting retrospectives. This case study examines some of the factors that contribute to a successful post-project review or retrospective.

WHY DO RETROSPECTIVES?

Retrospectives are primarily about learning. People come together to consider what worked well and what could have been done better on the project, with a view to achieving objectives such as:

- identifying improvements to project processes (say estimation or risk management), and hence documenting these for future projects;

- identifying potential improvements to the outputs created by the project, and hence feeding this information into future product development plans;

- identifying ways to improve the effectiveness of the project team, for example by strengthening communications or improving key practices and tools.

CONDUCTING A RETROSPECTIVE

Unstructured discussions, even if labelled 'brainstorming', tend to be fairly unproductive. A structured retrospective is far more likely to add value. This requires attention to planning, to managing the retrospective event itself and to subsequent information dissemination. Sounds just like a project? Let's look at each of those phases.

PLANNING

Given that it can be so hard to get people together for a retrospective, we want to ensure we use their time effectively. During the planning phase we may:

- Identify a facilitator: Retrospectives can range from multi-day events at the end of a major project to a couple of hours at the end of a two-week iteration. Regular, small retrospectives might be facilitated by a member of the project team. Larger events are likely to benefit from independent facilitation. In either case, someone needs to be identified to plan and conduct the event.

- Clarify the objectives: As with all reviews, we need to focus – we can't hope to cover everything within a limited timespan. Setting clear objectives helps us choose the appropriate participants and exercises.

- Identify participants: For example, are we focusing on the experience of the project team, or is it worthwhile inviting other stakeholders too? The objectives will help answer such questions.

- Understand the project culture: The facilitator may wish to observe the project's working areas, review documentation, and talk to team members in order to identify the types of exercises that will work best for this organization.

- Understand what happened on the project: Gathering materials such as metrics, an outline of key events, and so on, can help ground discussions in objective data. If an external facilitator is involved, then this data gathering also helps them get up to speed with the project.

- Interview participants: This helps understand their perspective on the project and the issues and concerns they might want to address during the retrospective. This information in turn informs the choice of structure and exercises for the event.

- Plan the event: Kerth (2001) and Derby and Larsen (2006) describe a range of exercises that can be used to kick off a retrospective, gather data about what happened during the project, and hence analyse and structure this data. The facilitator might choose a series of such activities centred on the retrospective's objectives.

- Manage logistics: Identify a location, plan the room layout, define the agenda, and so on. For a multi-day event, this can be a substantial exercise in itself.

- Brief the participants: As a minimum, they need to be advised of the objectives and logistics. It may also help to provide information such as an overview of the project, background on the retrospective process, and even preparatory questions or exercises to help them get into the right mindset for the retrospective.

Naturally the amount of effort put into planning depends on the scale of the retrospective. A small iteration review is unlikely, for example, to devote a lot of effort to interviewing participants.

RUNNING THE EVENT

Derby and Larsen (2006) identify five phases for a retrospective:

1. Setting the stage: The facilitator welcomes people, describes the objectives and structure of the retrospective, and discusses ground rules.

2. Gathering data: Participants bring together their perspectives to build a shared picture of what happened on the project. This includes hard data (metrics, dates of key events, and suchlike) and soft data (feelings and perceptions).

3. Generating insights: Identify trends and patterns in the data and hence try to build insight as to what caused things to happen the way they did.

4.   Deciding what to do: Prioritize the issues and opportunities identified during the retrospective, and hence plan what can be done to address them.

5.   Closing: Define how the findings and plans will be disseminated. Recap and wrap up the session.

At the same time, retrospectives should be seen as exploratory exercises. As they gather information about the project, the facilitator may need to restructure the agenda to accommodate the issues that are coming out.

DISSEMINATING THE RESULTS

This is another traditional weakness of post-project reviews. 'Lessons Learned' documents get written, filed and ignored. To address this dynamic, it's worth considering practices such as:

- Small, frequent retrospectives: Conducting a retrospective at the end of each phase, rather than at the end of the whole project, makes it easier to assemble the team. More importantly, the team can take the lessons learned from one phase and apply them immediately to the next phase. (This is especially true on highly iterative projects.)

- Focus on what 'we' can do, not what 'they' can do: Participants are much more likely to be committed to action than external people. If external action is needed, then the retrospective could focus on what the participants can do to build and communicate a case for this action.

- Manage benefits realization: Monitor the effects of actions identified during retrospectives. Having solid examples of these benefits will help build the case for senior managers to take broader actions in future.

- Disseminate findings through mentoring, review teams and other activities, not just through documents: Chapter 5 discusses how review teams can embed findings in checklists and other artefacts, thus helping to disseminate them throughout the organization. Other people (e.g. members of a PMO) may also be able to help disseminate findings.

- Do a retrospective of the retrospective: It's worth taking some time to think about what worked and what didn't, so that the retrospective process itself can be improved.

FACILITATING THE RETROSPECTIVE

Good facilitation is another success factor. Retrospectives may need to deal with widely differing perceptions of the project, team conflict, political agendas and other emotionally charged issues. A trained, independent facilitator can help navigate these issues. It may help if the facilitator has a solid understanding of the subject matter being addressed by the project, so they understand what people are saying, but their primary role is to manage the group process and structure of the retrospective, so that the team can focus on understanding what happened during the project.

CLOSING COMMENTS

Most of the above activities are relevant to all types of review. This emphasizes that retrospectives are just one type of project review, albeit one with a strong focus on team and organizational learning.

Reviews and Organizational Learning

Reviews help projects keep in touch with reality. This grounding in reality, as well as helping us to manage each project more effectively, is an important basis for personal, team and organizational learning. In order to learn from experience, we need first to have an accurate perception of what actually happened on our projects. Building from this base, reviews support learning in four ways:

1. providing space for reflection

2. creating an organizational memory

3. supporting dissemination of learning

4. building individual skills

This chapter looks at each of these four roles for reviews. In particular, it focuses on the feedback loop for organizational learning shown in Figure 3.1 (page 57), and the way review checklists can be managed in order to support this feedback.

PROVIDING SPACE FOR REFLECTION

We noted in Chapter 2 that reviews can provide a sounding board for people to discuss their experiences and perceptions. Many project teams find it difficult to create space to think and reflect – the pressures to act and appear busy are enormous in many organizations. Simply by being available to listen to people, reviewers make it easier for teams to reflect on their experience and hence learn. By listening actively, for example, by asking clarifying questions and drawing attention to inconsistencies in peoples' perceptions, reviewers can help teams think through what is actually going on and what the root cause for problems might be. This is an essential first step to identifying ways to improve.

If all reviews provide support for this process of reflection, then retrospectives and post-project reviews are particularly focused on capturing and learning from experience. As the case study *Post-Project Reviews and Retrospectives* shows, well-structured retrospectives provide a very active opportunity to explore what has happened on a project and hence define and prioritize potential improvements.

CREATING AN ORGANIZATIONAL MEMORY

The second feedback loop shown in Figure 3.1 (page 57), 'Feedback to improve reference models', takes this individual and team learning and embeds it in organizational memory. Reference models are a key part of this memory: as review teams incorporate the lessons learned on individual projects into their reference models, they make this knowledge available to other projects. Furthermore, review teams actively use the models whenever they conduct reviews. Projects are therefore far more likely to access this information than they are to read 'Lessons Learned' documents stored in a filing cabinet somewhere.

Thus, it is worthwhile building a way to update and maintain reference models into our review process. Retrospectives are the ideal way to do this. After each review, we might ask questions such as:

- Is the project doing anything that is worth sharing with other teams? If so, is it worth updating some aspect of our organizational standards, policies or guidelines to reflect this?

- Has the project run into any particular problems or issues that might be relevant to other projects? If so, could we include these in our reference models, for example, within risk identification checklists?

- Did we identify any issues with the project that weren't covered by our current review checklists? If so, what questions might we ask to draw out such issues?

- Are there any questions that we ask regularly but that don't uncover issues? These are candidates for removal from the review checklists. (Perhaps they were useful once, but the organization has now embedded ways to deal with them into its standard processes.)

- What did we learn from this review, and how can we modify our process, team structure, checklists or other models to reflect this learning?

These questions help to elicit refinements to two types of reference model: the general project management and related standards that apply across the organization, and the specific checklists and processes used by review teams. The balance of this section focuses on that second type of model.

BUILDING MEMORY THROUGH CHECKLISTS

Most review teams use checklists to identify questions they might ask, ensure they don't overlook issues, and tailor their investigations to specific stages of the project lifecycle. Beyond this common usage, three factors make checklists an especially useful way to capture experience, test its applicability to other projects and hence disseminate lessons learned more widely:

1. The barriers to maintaining them are relatively low. It's easy to insert a new question into a checklist. And, because the checklists are under the direct control of the reviewers who are using them, there is relatively little bureaucracy involved in making such changes.

2. The incentives to maintain them are relatively high. Reviewers derive direct benefit from having up-to-date checklists, so they have a strong incentive to maintain them.

3. The cycle time to refine and disseminate lessons learned via checklists is relatively short. As updates are made, reviewers can start testing them on other projects immediately. This spreads the lessons rapidly, and provides additional feedback to further refine them.

Review teams that actively manage their checklists through retrospectives and related feedback may start out with fairly generic lists of questions, but they will rapidly tailor these lists to focus on the issues that are important to their organization. In this way, the checklist becomes a repository recording the types of issue that commonly affect this organization. Then as the organization and the projects it undertakes evolve, so does the checklist.

CREATING USEFUL CHECKLISTS

There are a number of places to begin when creating our initial checklists. Several organizations have published questions they use when conducting reviews. (OGC, 2004b, is a good example). Tables 5.1 and 5.2 (pages 97 and 100 may also be useful). Organizational policies and standards are another potential starting point. Reviewers' personal experience will suggest other questions that are worth asking. However, all of these sources are only starting points: as described above, much of the value in a checklist comes from the organizational memory it contains.

Three other practical factors affect the value and utility of a checklist – the context in which it will be used, the balance of question types it contains and its length. Checklist questions may be used in a variety of contexts. For example:

- as part of an interview protocol;
- within self-assessment instruments;
- to guide document reviews;
- to support observation.

Some questions may be useful for several contexts. For example, it's common to analyse the responses to self-assessment questions in order to identify areas of divergence (or of suspicious degrees of convergence). These questions can then be probed in more depth during interviews. This means we may include a range of questions in a self-assessment checklist, then focus on a subset of these during interviews. Other questions will be useful only for specific purposes, things to look for when reviewing certain types of document, or when observing team areas for signs of stress. So as we gather and refine questions, we need to consider the context within which they will be useful.

Likewise, there are various different types of question that we can ask – closed, open and metaquestions. This repertoire comes fully into play during interviews, so we discuss it in detail in Chapter 6. However, when we create checklists it is worth considering the balance of specific versus open questions they contain:

- If there are specific issues that recur regularly on our projects, or that have a critical impact when they do occur, we want focused questions that will zero in on these issues quickly. These are often closed questions, ones that allow a simple answer such as 'yes' or 'no', or a specific date or metric. Such questions elicit unambiguous responses, and often allow statistical analysis of these responses.

- More open questions may elicit narrative responses. Such questions can be designed to bring out issues in a wider range of circumstances, but the responses need more manual analysis.

Long lists of highly specific questions may be easy to analyse, but they tend to elicit a box-checking mentality – people race through the checklist ticking boxes, without putting much thought into any question. A shorter checklist that mixes specific questions with more open-ended ones is more likely to be effective.

The sample checklist in Table 5.2 (pages 100–117) also contains a few metaquestions in its final section. These are designed to elicit additional questions and areas for investigation as their responses, and thus provide direct input to the process of refining our checklists. For example:

- *Are there any other questions that this review should be asking?* This allows the answerer to identify areas where they have concerns about the project, and gives us additional questions to consider for inclusion in the checklist.

- *What areas of advice or expertise would you like the review team to bring to the project?* This helps identify areas where the project team may lack skills. It may also provide hints as to what skills we need on our general reviewing pool.

Such questions may both bring out unanticipated issues on the project, and feed the project team's expertise into our design of checklists and the review process.

Finally, it is worth considering the length of our checklists. Long lists of questions, each of which identified an issue once upon a time on a project somewhere far away, are not especially useful. There isn't time to go through them in any meaningful way. Short checklists that cover the major issues that are likely to apply to the projects this organization is currently undertaking are much more effective. In this context, short probably means about two pages.

In order to manage the length of their checklists, some teams operate a 'one in, one out' policy. Whenever they add a new question to a checklist, they remove one that hasn't helped identify project issues recently. This focuses the mind on maximizing the utility of each question. An alternative approach is to maintain a database of questions, selecting a subset of them (determined by the review's objectives) for any specific review.

Metrics can be useful to guide this process. Gilb and Graham (1993), for example, describe a process that uses metrics to measure the utility of questions and hence determine which ones might be included in checklists. This introduces a degree of rigour, but relies on you conducting a sufficiently large number of reviews for the statistics to be meaningful. (Such metrics can be backed by a database recording the issues identified by reviews and linking them to the questions that identified them. As well as supporting the selection and retirement of questions, such a database allows analysis of issue frequency and trends. This provides information to monitor the benefits generated by reviews, and to support wider process improvement initiatives.)

STARTING POINTS – SOME USEFUL CHECKLISTS

Tables 5.1 and 5.2 contain checklists I use when reviewing projects. These may provide useful starting points for your own reviews.

Table 5.1 (page 97) contains fairly general questions that help identify signs of stress on a project. Many such signs are probably instinctive as much as they're conscious: this is why people talk about 'bad smells'. Likewise, at least some of them will be environment-specific. Every organization and type of project will probably exhibit stress in its own characteristic way.

Table 5.2 (pages 100–117) contains a checklist of technical questions I use when reviewing systems development projects. All of the caveats of the above sections apply. The checklist is focused on a specific context (self-assessments and interview protocols for projects developing online systems), and I would typically use only a subset of the questions (determined by the project stage) for any single review. Nonetheless, it illustrates the types of question that may be worth including in a checklist.

Of course, knowing what to look for is one thing. Actually seeing it and gathering evidence to convince others is another. The process of gathering such evidence is discussed in Chapter 6.

DISSEMINATING LEARNING

Even when they do capture 'Lessons Learned' at the end of their projects, many organizations find it difficult to disseminate those lessons more widely. As described above, capturing these lessons into review checklists and other reference models builds in a dissemination process: review teams will use the models whenever they conduct reviews, hence bringing these lessons to other projects.

Review teams are also well placed to disseminate knowledge through personal networking. Reviewers may act as mentors for project managers and team members, or they may put project teams directly in touch with each other ('Project X is also having problems like this, so their project manager will be able to give you some tips'). Both routes tend to be far more effective ways of disseminating knowledge than writing and filing a 'Lessons Learned' document.

One practical factor affects this dissemination process: version control on checklists and reference models. If these are being updated regularly and used across a number of review teams, then some mechanism to ensure that each team has access to the latest version is required. Web-based systems for collaborative document management can be ideal for this.

BUILDING INDIVIDUAL SKILLS

Reviews are an excellent way for people to broaden their experience and skills. Beyond the opportunity to reflect on their own projects, reviews can help people develop their skills in a variety of ways:

1. Exposure to a range of different projects: By participating in review teams, people see a range of different projects and approaches. This is a good way to broaden their experience. Some organizations (e.g. see the case study *Assuring Fixed Price Implementations*) specifically include junior people on review teams, together with more experienced reviewers, in order to give them experience in this way.

2. Exercising new skills: Participating in review teams also gives people the opportunity to exercise a range of skills, in areas such as interviewing and observation, analysing information and writing reports. Reviewers must also develop ways to assess new situations rapidly and hence identify appropriate options and recommendations. Finally, project reviews often happen at times of relatively high stress on a project (e.g. before major milestones) and reviewers are frequently perceived to be in an adversarial role.

This offers ample opportunity for reviewers to develop skills in diplomacy and conflict resolution.

3.   Receiving mentoring from reviewers: Project managers and team members can benefit from mentoring by reviewers, hence developing their skills in a range of project management and related areas. Likewise, members of review teams may benefit from working with specialists in areas such as finance, procurement, contracts and technical disciplines.

4.   Providing mentoring to project teams. Reviewers also gain by acting as mentors. In order to communicate clearly to their mentees, they often need to reflect on their experience and clarify their own thinking. This helps to consolidate and reinforce the lessons they have learned.

Organizations benefit from this learning in two ways. First, the general level of skills within the organization is raised. Second, knowledge of the organization's projects and techniques is spread more widely. This provides added resilience in the face of staff turnover and increased capacity to divert resources between projects when necessary.

BUILDING A LEARNING ORGANIZATION

Many organizations frame reviews as a control mechanism, a way to ensure that their projects are under control. This chapter suggests an alternative and potentially more powerful framing: reviews as a way to enhance and accelerate organizational learning. People need feedback in order to learn. By creating effective feedback loops within and between projects, reviews can be a very effective way to increase overall organizational effectiveness.

Table 5.1 Some signs of project stress

Communications
• Are people reluctant to discuss certain areas of the project, or do they give evasive or scripted/overly consistent answers? • Are people reluctant to give access to work products and prototypes, or do they only allow carefully scripted demonstrations of systems and suchlike? • Are there any gaps in communication patterns? For example, failure to consult important stakeholders; cliques and factions within project teams; key team members who are too busy to talk with other members of the team? • Note the general tenor of discussion and meetings. For example, is it relaxed and confident, or are there frequent, heated and hastily convened meetings to address issues?
Inconsistencies
• Do people have a consistent understanding of project objectives, deliverables, schedules, quality standards and so on? Is this understanding consistent with the objectives in the project's documentation? • Are there inconsistencies within or between documents? • Are people working from inconsistent or out-of-date versions of documents?
Changes
• Are the assumptions behind the business case, project plan, schedules, budgets, and other assets still valid? Have there been any other changes to the project team, organization or external environment that affect the project? How are these changes being monitored? • How did these assets change as they were created? For example, were there areas that changed frequently, perhaps because of uncertainties or disagreements within the team? Is the rationale for key decisions documented and accepted? Are there any signs that key elements of these rationales have now changed? • How frequently are project plans, risk registers and suchlike changing? (If they're not changing, then perhaps they're not being used? If they're changing very frequently, then how well founded are they and their underlying assumptions?) • How are changes to scope and requirements being managed and communicated?
Team stress
• Look for signs such as long working hours, excessively untidy offices, frequent outbursts of anger. Cultures vary, but in general if the team is acting stressed, then the project is probably stressed. Even if the project is fine at this point, stressed people tend to make more mistakes. (In many organizations, such stress will not in itself be seen as something that needs fixing. However, if you see stress you should also be looking for signs of its impact.) • Are there signs of poor or declining morale, excessive team turnover or suchlike? Do the project sponsor's and manager's assessments of morale match those made by of people on the project team?

Table 5.1   *Continued*

Project infrastructure
<ul><li>Does everyone have the tools and equipment they need?</li><li>Are people spending time working around gaps in processes or tool availability?</li><li>Are processes such as configuration management, build management and release management well defined? Do they operate smoothly? How frequently do people need to fix issues as a result of failures in these processes?</li><li>Are people putting a lot of effort into basic administrative processes – booking meeting rooms, finding and managing documents, time recording, and so on?</li><li>Is there sufficient meeting space? Or are people meeting in inappropriate places, walking long distances to meeting rooms or putting off meetings? (Teams typically need a mix of formal and informal meeting areas, for scheduled meetings and ad hoc discussions respectively. Is there a mix of such spaces?)</li><li>Projects in trouble often lack well-oiled support processes – they spend time firefighting rather than building infrastructure. This leads to people's time being siphoned off into basic administrative and support processes. As well as being a sign of stress, this can point at areas where relatively small improvements can have a big impact on the project. (Some projects have the converse problem: too much effort invested in building project infrastructure and tools, with insufficient attention to delivering the project.)</li></ul>
Project management processes and controls
<ul><li>Are the criteria for signing off milestones or deliverables clear? Have milestones or deliverables been signed off without fully meeting these criteria? (It's easy for a team to fool itself by saying: 'Well, we almost achieved the criteria and we'd done extra work somewhere else.')</li><li>Are the assumptions behind estimates and resource allocations clear? Are they well founded? Do they still hold? (e.g. are they consistent with the project's recent progress? Are the assumed resources actually available?)</li><li>Have schedules and plans been developed to an appropriate level of granularity? Are they being maintained? What is the rate of change to the plans? Are dependencies clear? Are key dependencies being monitored?</li><li>How is status against these plans being tracked? Is actual performance data being used to refine estimates and plans for future progress? Do status reports clearly reflect actual progress and issues? How are variances between planned and actual progress being managed (both to address immediate variances and to find and address root causes)? Is the project currently on course to achieve its goals, both in terms of time and budget and in the quality of the deliverables?</li><li>Are processes for risk and issue management, change control, configuration management, quality management and suchlike clear and well understood by all relevant people? Are people following these processes? Are there any areas where these processes are falling down?</li><li>Is there a well-defined communication plan? Is this plan being followed? Are people getting the information they need, when they need it?</li><li>Are key documents or databases out of date? For example, risk registers that haven't been updated recently; teams using local plans because the centrally managed plan is out of date?</li><li>Good project managers will normally have these things reasonably well under control, and even weak project managers will know how to give the 'right' answer to most of the above questions. So reviewers often add most value by looking for signs of incipient failures and by gently probing for evidence to back up (or refute) the answers.</li></ul>

Table 5.1   *Concluded*

Organizational patterns
• Most organizations have common failure patterns. Because of the style of project they do, their culture, and so on, they make similar mistakes across many projects. Review teams are often well placed to recognize these issues, capture them into checklists, and hence to begin to identify and address the common causes beneath these failures.

Table 5.2 Sample review checklist

	Self-assessment (include references to supporting documents where appropriate)	Review notes	Actions (including owner and date)	RAG
1. Scope and objectives				
1 **Objectives** • What are the overall objectives for this programme? • How does your project contribute to these objectives?	Project team records its self-assessment in this column	Review team records its assessment in this column, considering questions such as:	Record actions identified during the course of the review	Record Red/ Amber/ Green status for this aspect
2 **Deliverables** • What must you deliver in order to achieve those project objectives? • What items have been explicitly identified as being out of scope?		• Do all stakeholders have a consistent perception/ understanding of this aspect of the project? Is this understanding consistent with the project's documentation?		
3 **Sign-off** • How will you assess the completeness of those deliverables? • Who needs to be involved in this process?		• Is this understanding consistent with the review team's observations? • Is this understanding consistent with broader organizational objectives and standards?		
4 **Trade-offs** • What trade-offs have been made in order to define those deliverables (e.g. have you dropped functionality in order to achieve deadlines, or have you compromised on elements such as security, scalability or user interface design)? • How have these trade-offs been communicated to all stakeholders?		• How has this aspect of the project changed since project inception? Since the last review?		

Table 5.2 *Continued*

5 Ownership • Is there a detailed checklist of deliverables (e.g. scope matrix) with clearly identified ownership and delivery milestones for each deliverable?					
6 Completeness • How will the completeness (including quality assessment) of each item on that checklist be assessed? • How will any disputes about completeness be resolved?					
7 Risks • Which deliverables will be most difficult to create? • Why are they difficult, and what will you do to reduce this difficulty?					
8 Change • How have the above items changed since the last review? (Outline key changes here, and capture details into the boxes above.)					
9 Milestones achieved • What milestones have been achieved since the last review? • How was completeness of these milestones assessed • Have all relevant parties signed them off?					
10 Milestones missed • What milestones have been missed since the last review? • What impact has this had on the overall plans? • How will the impact of these changes be managed?					
11 Velocity • What has your velocity been since the last review? • How does this compare with the velocity you expected to achieve, and what implications does that have for the balance of the project?					

Table 5.2 *Continued*

		Self-assessment (include references to supporting documents where appropriate)	Review notes	Actions (including owner and date)	RAG
12	**Actions** • Have all actions from the last review been performed? • How will any outstanding actions be handled?				
2. Project management and planning					
1	**Plans** • Do you have a high-level plan for the entire project? • Do you have detailed plans for the next phase (e.g. next 4–6 weeks)?				
2	**Milestones** • Are key milestones defined? • Is there at least one milestone each month? • How will the completeness of these milestones be assessed? • When will independent reviews be conducted?				
3	**Velocity** • If using an iterative approach, how will the velocity of each iteration be assessed, and how will this be used to set expectations for future iterations & deliverables?				
4	**Work breakdown** • How does the work breakdown structure marry to deliverables and milestones – do you understand which tasks relate to which deliverable?				
5	**Stability** • How stable are the plans and estimates? • Which areas are still undergoing most change?				

Table 5.2 *Continued*

6	**Internal dependencies** • Are all dependencies within the project plan defined and understood? • How will these dependencies be monitored and managed?			
7	**External dependencies** • Are all dependencies on external parties and systems defined? • How will these dependencies be monitored and managed?			
8	**Estimates** • What is the basis for your estimates (of time, cost, effort, etc.)? • What level of granularity (in terms of tasks, components, or other artefacts) supports these estimates? • How is the 'doneness' of each artefact defined? • Where do your metrics (e.g. for time to complete a specific task) come from? • What provision for 'overheads' (e.g. team meetings and communication) is made?			
9	**Progress tracking** • How will you track progress during the project?			
10	**Communications** • Have all internal and external stakeholders been identified? • Has a communications plan for the project been created? • How will status and issues be communicated within the team and to external stakeholders? • What regular meetings, conference calls, status reports, etc. will be required? • How will differences in time zone, language, etc. be handled?			

Table 5.2 *Continued*

	Self-assessment (include references to supporting documents where appropriate)	Review notes	Actions (including owner and date)	RAG
11	**Information radiators** • What 'information radiators' do you plan to use? • How will these be created, disseminated and updated?			
12	**Escalation** • How will issues be escalated?			
13	**Change management** • How will changes to objectives, requirements, external dependencies, etc. be managed during the project?			
14	**Review** • What peer or independent reviews of plans, progress, design, code, etc. will be conducted during the project? • How will issues identified by these reviews be addressed?			
15	**Risks** • How will risks be identified and mitigated during the project? • What are currently seen as the key risks for the project, and how are these being managed? • Which type of risk (e.g. technical, external dependency, relationship) is most likely to affect you?			
16	**Issues** • Are there any open issues? • How are these being tracked and managed?			
17	**Change** • How have the above items changed since the last review? (Outline key changes here, and capture details into the boxes above.)			

Table 5.2 *Continued*

18	**Actions** • Have all actions from the last review been performed? • How will any outstanding actions be handled?					
3. Requirements						
1	**Definition** • How are the functional requirements defined (e.g. use cases, stories, wire frames)? • How much detail do these definitions contain and in what format? • How complete and consistent are they?					
2	**Sign-off** • Have the requirements been reviewed? • Who has signed them off? • Have all key stakeholders (buyers, users, system operators, etc.) been involved?					
3	**Change** • How stable are the requirements? • What are main areas of change or uncertainty? • How will ongoing change be managed?					
4	**Risk** • What are the main areas of risk in the requirements (e.g. because they are not yet fully understood, are still changing, or you are unclear how to implement them)? • How will this risk be managed?					
5	**Testability** • How easy will it be to test whether the requirements have been delivered? • Are there any areas that will be particularly difficult to test?					

Table 5.2 *Continued*

	Self-assessment (include references to supporting documents where appropriate)	Review notes	Actions (including owner and date)	RAG
6 User interaction • If you are relying on frequent user interaction to refine requirements throughout development, have appropriate users been identified and dedicated to the project?				
7 Domain model • Do you have a clear understanding of the domain model for this application (e.g. what are the key entities and how do they relate to each other)?				
8 Security • Are there any special requirements regarding security? • Who's responsible for delivering the security 'infrastructure' for the system (e.g. network and physical security, identity and authorization systems, application security)? • Has this infrastructure been designed? • Is penetration test or other security review planned? • Are requirements for audit trails, authentication and identity management, etc. understood? • How will sign-off that these requirements have been met be obtained?				
9 Performance • Do we have clearly defined and measurable criteria for volumetrics, performance and scalability of the system? • How challenging are these requirements? • How will we assess whether the system meets these criteria?				

Table 5.2 *Continued*

10	**Maintainability** • What aspects of the system are most likely to change in future (i.e. after the initial system goes live)? • Who will perform this maintenance? • Have they reviewed the design, and are they happy that they will be able to support such changes? • How will they get up to speed with the system, e.g. what is the handover process?				
11	**Operations** • Have requirements for service introduction, data migration, operability and related concerns been defined? • What are the criteria for accepting the system into live operations?				
12	**Resilience** • Have requirements for system resilience and recoverability, redundancy, disaster recovery, etc. been defined? • How will we assure that these requirements have been met?				
13	**Traceability** • How will we ensure that the systems as designed and built will deliver all the requirements?				
14	**Change** • How have the above items changed since the last review? (Outline key changes here, and capture details into the boxes above.)				
15	**Actions** • Have all actions from the last review been performed? • How will any outstanding actions be handled?				

Table 5.2 *Continued*

	Self-assessment (include references to supporting documents where appropriate)	Review notes	Actions (including owner and date)	RAG
4. User experience design				
1 User groups • Have you identified all user groups that will interact with the system (either as primary users or in support roles such as admin and maintenance)? • How well do you understand their objectives and win conditions?				
2 Interfaces • Have you identified all user interfaces to the system (screens, pages, devices, reports, training manuals, etc.)? • How precisely have these been delimited and what is the current state of design of each interface (e.g. have all usage scenarios been defined, are wireframes complete for all pages, have visual design standards been agreed, have management reports been defined)?				
3 Processes • Have processes associated with maintaining elements of the system (e.g. editorial and content management workflows) been defined and all associated roles and responsibilities identified?				
4 Prototypes • Have you constructed prototypes (low- or high-fidelity) for key screens and tested these with target users?				
5 Testing • Will usability, accessibility or other testing be conducted on the final system? If so, how will this be performed?				

Table 5.2 *Continued*

6 Sign-off • What is the process for signing off the user experience (UE) design? • How will changes be accommodated as they occur through the project?				
7 Change • How have the above items changed since the last review? (Outline key changes here, and capture details into the boxes above.)				
8 Actions • Have all actions from the last review been performed? How will any outstanding actions be handled?				
5. Technical architecture and design				
1 Architecture • Has the overall architecture for the system been defined (e.g. as views of the application, technical and physical architecture)? If so, describe the key elements of it. If not, how will you define the architecture and when will this be done by?				
2 Standards • Does the architecture align to wider architectural standards within the organization (e.g. will any variations or special considerations be required to support this architecture)?				
3 Interfaces • How are key external interfaces defined? • Do you understand the data that will flow across such interfaces (format, protocols, volumetrics, security requirements, etc.)? • Have you reviewed your designs for interface-handlers with the relevant external system owners? • How will you communicate with these system owners throughout the project?				

Table 5.2 *Continued*

	Self-assessment (include references to supporting documents where appropriate)	Review notes	Actions (including owner and date)	RAG
4 Components • How has the system been partitioned into subsystems/components? • Do you have detailed designs for each component? If so, how have these been documented (give examples)? If not, how will detailed designs be developed?				
5 Sign-off • Has the architecture and design been reviewed? • Who by? • Does it need to be approved by any other parties? If so, how will this approval be obtained?				
6 Traceability • How is the design mapped back to the original requirements to ensure that there are no gaps?				
7 Non-functional requirements • How will you demonstrate that the design meets the non-functional requirements (e.g. performance, security, maintainability)?				
8 Operational requirements • Are there any special requirements for introducing the system into service (e.g. data and user migration), or for subsequent operations? • How does the design accommodate these requirements?				

Table 5.2 *Continued*

9 Change • What areas of the design are still changing? • What impact is such change likely to have on implementation? • How will changes to requirements or design be managed throughout the balance of the project?		
10 Risks • Which are the areas of highest technical risk in the system (e.g. complex or new technologies, tight requirements)? • How will these risks be mitigated (e.g. have you developed prototypes to explore and buy information about the risks)?		
11 Change • How have the above items changed since the last review? (Outline key changes here, and capture details into the boxes above.)		
12 Actions • Have all actions from the last review been performed? • How will any outstanding actions be handled?		
6. Development		
1 Approach • Describe the overall approach to development (e.g. team organization, phases and iterations).		
2 Languages and tools • What languages and tools will you be using for development? • Are all the necessary tools in place already? • What level of skills and experience does the team have with these tools?		

Table 5.2   Continued

	Self-assessment (include references to supporting documents where appropriate)	Review notes	Actions (including owner and date)	RAG
3 Skills • Is the team in place? • Do they have the complete set of skills required to execute the project? • Which skills are most critical to success?				
4 Progress tracking • How will you track progress during development? • How will you monitor team 'velocity' and use this to refine plans?				
5 Quality management • How will you monitor the quality of deliverables?				
6 Support • What environments and other supporting infrastructure will you need during development? • Are these in place? • Are supporting processes (e.g. for regular build and integration and smoke test) defined?				
7 Third parties • Which people outside the project team will you need to interact with during development cycles? • How will these communications be managed?				
8 Risks • What are the most risky areas for development? • How will you manage these risks?				

Table 5.2 *Continued*

9 **Change** • How have the above items changed since the last review? (Outline key changes here, and capture details into the boxes above.)			
10 **Actions** • Have all actions from the last review been performed? • How will any outstanding actions be handled?			
7. Testing			
1 **Approach** • What is the overall approach to testing (e.g. what phases of testing will be performed; how will tests be planned and defined)?			
2 **Estimates and timing** • How have you derived your estimates of the effort and elapsed time required for testing?			
3 **Coverage** • How will test coverage be measured? • How do your effort estimates balance coverage with cost? • What is the proportion of scripted versus exploratory testing in this coverage?			
4 **Roles and responsibilities** • Who is responsible for which aspects of testing (e.g. unit, integration, system and acceptance test; test design, development and execution; functional and non-functional testing)?			

Table 5.2 *Continued*

	Self-assessment (include references to supporting documents where appropriate)	Review notes	Actions (including owner and date)	RAG
5 Sign-offs • What are the entry and exit criteria to each stage of testing, and how will these criteria be assessed? • What sign-offs will be required and who is responsible for them?				
6 Progress tracking • How will you track the progress and completeness of test and defect-fixing?				
7 Environments • What test environments will you need, and how will configuration management (e.g. promotion of code) across these environments be managed? • How will you test interactions with external systems?				
8 Tools and metrics • What tools will you use to perform testing and track test and defect/issue status? • What metrics will you be using? • What tools will you use to support test-driven development or other automated testing? • Does the team have adequate skills with these tools?				
9 Fix and retest • How will diagnosis, fix and retest of defects be handled? • How do your effort estimates accommodate this cycle?				
10 Data • What test data will be required, and where will this data come from?				

Table 5.2 *Continued*

11 Risks • What are the key risks to successful execution of appropriate testing for this project?			
12 Change • How have the above items changed since the last review? (Outline key changes here, and capture details into the boxes above.)			
13 Actions • Have all actions from the last review been performed? • How will any outstanding actions be handled?			
8. Service introduction and operations			
1 Live environment • How will the live environment (e.g. physical hosting facilities, servers & networks, operating systems and databases) be set up for the system?			
2 Service introduction • What is the process for introducing the system into live operations? • What sign-offs are needed, who will make them and what criteria will they use?			
3 Operations • What operational requirements must the system meet (e.g. for backup and system admin; for data and user admin), and how will it meet them? • Who will be responsible for performing these operational tasks once the system is live?			

Table 5.2 *Continued*

		Self-assessment (include references to supporting documents where appropriate)	Review notes	Actions (including owner and date)	RAG
4	**Maintenance** • Who will be responsible for maintaining the system (e.g. defect diagnosis and fixing; extension and refinement of the system) once it is live?				
5	**Knowledge transfer** • How will the development team transfer knowledge to the people performing operations and maintenance? • What documentation, training, shadowing, etc. is required? • What user training is required? • Who is responsible for this?				
6	**Tools** • What management tools must the system interface to in live operations (e.g. for event logging, audit trails, system management)? • Are the interfaces to these tools defined?				
7	**Risks** • What are the key risks to successful service introduction and operations of the system?				
8	**Change** • How have the above items changed since the last review? (Outline key changes here, and capture details into the boxes above.)				
9	**Actions** • Have all actions from the last review been performed? • How will any outstanding actions be handled?				

Table 5.2   *Concluded*

9. Other				
1	**Third Parties** • What other contractors or third parties are involved with the project, and how will they be managed? • What are the key dependencies and risks associated with these third parties?			
2	**Other Concerns** • Are there any other areas of the project that you are particularly concerned about?			
3	**Review coverage** • Are there any areas that this review should be covering, not addressed in the above questions?			
4	**Review support** *What areas of advice or expertise would you like the review team to bring to the project?*			
5	**Review focus** • Where do you think the review team should focus their attention?			
6	**Change** • How have the above items changed since the last review? (Outline key changes here, and capture details into the boxes above.)			
7	**Actions** • Have all actions from the last review been performed? How will any outstanding actions be handled?			

CASE STUDY
Weeding the Project Portfolio

It's hard to kill a project. It brings people face-to-face with the possibility that they aren't as capable as they thought they were. For some people, it means that they have nothing to show for months or even years of effort. It may damage their reputation in the eyes of their peers and competitors. People may be angry about wasted investment, or scared by the possibility that they'll lose their job. Even when intellectually we know that we're managing a portfolio of risky investments, some of which won't pay off, handling this emotional fallout can be tough.

As a consequence, many organizations are very bad at killing projects. It tends to be a lot easier to let a project drift, consuming budget and resources, than to call a halt. We defer the pain, hoping in the true spirit of Charles Dickens's Mr Micawber that 'something will turn up' (Dickens, 2004[1850]) to rescue the project.

Going back to the case study that opened this book, *Earthquakes in the Project Portfolio*, that was certainly my experience in the games industry. Intellectually, it was fairly clear that our projects fell into three classes:

- Hits: Perhaps 10 per cent of the portfolio, or six games out of the 60 under development at any time, would be outrageous successes. These would deliver returns on investment of 200 per cent or more.

- Break even: The next 80 per cent of the portfolio would eventually deliver a credible but not especially noteworthy game. On average, such games might cover their development costs, give or take a little.

- Disasters: The final six projects would never deliver anything credible. Even if they did actually complete the game, it'd be too dire to take to market.

In such an environment, there's a clear path to business success: maximize your marketing investment in the hits, tweak the break-even projects to improve quality and reduce costs, and kill the disasters as quickly as possible.

As project reviewers, we could do little to help recognize the hits. (Fortunately, decisions on marketing investment could be deferred until well into development.) We could, however, recognize several signs of incipient disaster. Some projects would regularly defer deliverables, pushing milestones later and later into the schedule. They'd showcase the same artwork month after month. The project team might gradually lose all sense of urgency and purpose, or it might operate in a constant state of adrenaline and firefighting. Either way, their ability to take action to improve the project would be seriously impaired. Some projects eventually delivered a credible game despite all these signs, but many didn't.

We found it very hard to deal with these projects. Their executive owners were in fierce competition with each other, so they tended to become very defensive whenever someone raised questions about one of 'their' projects. If we called attention to a project before we had clear evidence that it was in trouble, we created a standoff. The project owner would defend the project vigorously, building an entrenched position that meant we would ultimately need even more evidence before gaining their commitment to reshape or kill the project. In the meantime, dealing with such a combative project owner could be very stressful for the review team.

After we went round this loop a number of times, we learned to spend several months building a clear case before we called for action. This case might, for example, include independent quality reviews of the game's code and artwork, or examples of three or more status reports all claiming the same deliverables as evidence of progress. It could be frustrating to see a project burning money while we painstakingly gathered evidence, but it was necessary.

Here's what I learned from this experience:

- Gathering evidence is hard work, and it takes time.

- Many organizations have an asymmetric need for evidence. They may initiate projects on the basis of partial information and gut feel, but they will only reshape or kill projects when the evidence is very clear. (Initiation is a positive act, whereas killing a project runs into far more negative emotions.)

- The amount of evidence you need to gather in order to trigger action will depend on your credibility and organizational context. As you build a reputation for making good calls, for example, the need for a full evidential chain may decrease.

- Conversely, if you call for action before you have sufficient evidence, then you risk driving opposition into an entrenched position. This simply raises the amount of evidence you need to gather. And dealing with entrenched opposition can be very unpleasant.

- If we could have triggered earlier action, we would certainly have saved our company significant sums of money. With earlier intervention, we would also have had more options, so we might even have reshaped some failed projects into at least partial successes. This creates a pressure to act before you have gathered all the evidence.

- Many executive owners argued that killing a project would damage staff morale. In practice, morale often went up when a struggling project was cancelled. Most people knew in their hearts that their project was going nowhere, and no-one likes working on a pointless project.

Evidence is important for all decisions. It needs to be gathered carefully and used wisely. Many factors influence the amount of evidence you need: the credibility of the assurance team, organizational politics and power structures, your relationship with the various stakeholders. Reviewers who aren't sensitive to all these factors will struggle to trigger effective action.

The Importance of Evidence

CHAPTER

6

Evidence is at the heart of a review. Unless we can gather clear evidence of what's actually happening on the project, we will have little hope of persuading people to act on our findings. And rightly so: if we don't have clear evidence, then how can we be sure our findings are well founded? Of course, clear objectives, agreed reference models, relevant checklists, and so on, are all important, but only because they guide the evidence-gathering process. This chapter looks at that process and some of the techniques it employs.

THE NEED FOR EVIDENCE

Evidence backs our findings and recommendations in three important ways:

- Understanding: People need sufficient information to understand what we're saying. To do this, we need to build a clear picture of the project's background and current state, of the issues that it's facing and of the likely impact of these issues. We also need to build a clear chain of reasoning from these observations to the underlying root causes and hence to our recommendations. (We may also need to clarify terminology and provide support for non-specialists to understand it, but that's a separate issue.)

- Acceptance: People may need additional information in order to believe what we're saying. For example, they may need independent verification of certain details, or sufficient data to demonstrate that trends are statistically meaningful, or confirmation by accepted experts that recommendations are well founded. Providing this information is especially important when our findings are contentious or when they challenge fundamental assumptions or expectations within our audience.

- Action: Finally, people may need different information again in order to act on what we're saying. For example, whereas our findings and recommendations may be based on trends and clusters of issues, people may need a detailed picture of the specific issues and where and when they are occurring in order to address them, and to track the effectiveness of their actions.

In each case, different people may need different levels of detail and different types of information. Some people only want the executive summary, while others thrive on as much detail as we can give them. Some people find numbers and metrics compelling. Others are more likely to believe diagrams. Others again will pay most attention to quotes and personal testimony from people on the project team. As we interact with stakeholders during the review, we need to look for signs as to what sort of information they prefer: this will help us to gather evidence and frame our findings appropriately. (This is also an area we should discuss with the review's sponsor as we negotiate our terms of reference.)

Several other factors influence the amount and type of evidence that we need to gather:

- The reputation of the review team: If reviewers are trusted by other stakeholders, the burden of evidence they require is likely to be lower. (Reviewers need to maintain their reputation, however. This means gathering sufficient evidence to assure themselves that their findings are well founded. It's easy enough for any team to overlook important facts or slip into groupthink under deadline and other pressures.)

- The size, complexity and importance of the project: It's easier to overlook or misunderstand important facts on large, complex programmes. The impact of mistakes is greater on mission-critical projects. In such cases, it makes sense to require a higher standard of evidence.

- The significance of the issues identified by the review team: Recommendations for substantial or contentious changes need to be backed by appropriate evidence.

- The degree of urgency of the issues: Gathering detailed evidence takes time. In some cases it may be necessary to act on partial information. (The case study *Weeding the Project Portfolio* touches on the dangers of trying to act with insufficient evidence.)

- The political situation: Some review teams operate in politically charged environments (see the case study *Review Techniques in the Education Sector*: school inspections are a highly charged subject and hence inspection teams must gather evidence carefully) or in situations where litigation is pending or threatened. This raises the standard of evidence which is required.

Review teams need to balance these factors against the available budget and the potential benefits of investing resources elsewhere. In some cases, for example, we may have bad feelings about a project but it's simply not important enough to justify gathering the evidence needed to clarify our intuition. Instead, we might let the project proceed until the issues become clearer of their own accord.

THE ANALYSIS LOOP

How do we gather this evidence? Figure 3.1 (page 57) shows an analysis loop at the core of the review process. Figure 6.1 (page 126) expands this loop to show three stages to gathering evidence:

1. Gathering raw data: We read documents, conduct interviews, analyse plans and deliverables, and so on. This gives us the basic data to build a picture of what is happening on the project.

2. Structuring this data: We search for patterns and trends in the data. We look for inconsistencies both within the data itself and by comparison to our reference models. As we do this, we identify issues and begin to classify and cluster them.

3. Generating hypotheses: We postulate underlying problems and root causes that might be driving the observed issues and trends. This in turn may lead to additional data gathering in order to clarify these underlying factors.

This model frames evidence gathering as a process of hypothesis testing: as we go around the loop, we generate hypotheses about the project and gather the data needed to confirm or refute these hypotheses. In doing this, we automatically gather the evidence needed to back up our findings and recommendations. (Hammersley and Atkinson (1995) discuss the relationship between observation and hypothesis testing in the context of ethnographic studies. Framing a review as an ethnographic study of the project gives many useful insights to the evidence gathering process.)

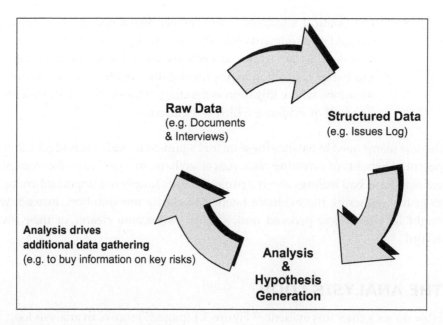

Figure 6.1   The analysis loop

The process is drawn as a loop, with no explicit starting point. Sometimes we will start with hypotheses. For example, the review may have been initiated because the sponsor is concerned about some aspect of the project. We will then be seeking data to test the reality underlying this concern. Or our organization may regularly experience certain issues on projects, and we will be checking whether any of these issues apply to this particular project. Every question in a checklist embeds hypotheses about issues that may be affecting the project. (OFSTED inspections, discussed in the *Reviews in the Education Sector* case study, are explicitly framed to begin with hypotheses.)

Other times we will start with data gathering. We try to keep our minds open as we observe the project and gather data about its progress, processes, communication patterns, deliverables, and so on. Hypotheses then emerge from this data. (In practice, observing 'everything' is difficult: we will probably focus in certain areas. Framing the process as hypothesis testing at least forces us to be explicit about, and hence to manage, these potential biases.)

ITERATION PLANNING

The analysis loop also emphasizes that reviews tend to be iterative. As we learn from the initial data we gather, we may identify other areas for investigation.

For example, during our initial interviews we may hear of additional people we need to talk to in order to understand an issue and clarify the facts behind it.

This being the case, it helps to plan for iteration from the outset. Considerations here include:

- Balancing breadth and depth: When conducting 'general' reviews (e.g. focusing on objectives and risks, as discussed earlier), we need to gain an overview across the entire project while also going into sufficient depth to convincingly describe the key issues. This can be handled by scheduling an initial broad iteration to assess the project and identify potential issues, followed by one or more focused iterations, each addressing a specific issue.

- Managing dependencies: There is often a natural order in which to review aspects of the project. For example, requirements might be reviewed in order to establish the baseline for design. Or we may want to review the quality and completeness of key deliverables before we review the status of the overall project. These dependencies will inform our iteration planning.

- Clarifying and confirming data: There is almost always scope to follow up our initial data gathering – we need to clarify things people say to us during interviews, talk to other people our interviewees refer us to, examine metrics and logs to explore the reality behind people's perceptions, and so on. It makes sense to schedule some time to do this.

On a major review, these iterations would probably be fairly formal, perhaps with scheduled checkpoints to review each iteration and plan the next. On smaller reviews, they might be less formal. Either way, considering the number and type of iterations helps us plan our time and resources.

ISSUES LOG

I find it useful to record the information gathered during the analysis loop into a central issues log (see Table 6.1 for an example), typically managed as a spreadsheet or small database for each review. As we examine documents and conduct interviews, we record any questions, inconsistencies, risks or other issues into this log, with a reference back to their source (e.g. the original document or interview notes). This structure helps in several ways:

- It brings all the potential issues into a single place, making subsequent analysis and pattern recognition easier.

- It helps trace classes of issues back to the original raw data. As we classify and cluster issues, we record this into the relevant column (or columns – it is sometimes useful to classify issues against multiple axes). Thus we have a trail from cluster to issue and hence to the original source.

- It can be extended easily. On more complex reviews, we may build models of the relationships between clusters of issues, perhaps capturing causal relationships and interdependencies. These can be captured in additional columns, retaining traceability to the original data.

- In environments where protecting the confidentiality of interviewees is important, it helps anonymize the issues. We can strip off the leading columns before delivering the log to the review's sponsor (while retaining the Issue ID for any future follow up with the original source).

A central log is particularly useful on large reviews where reviewers may be operating in parallel strands. However, I find the discipline of structuring my analysis in this way useful even on small reviews: it helps me organize my notes and separate raw data from inference and hypothesis.

Table 6.1   Issues log structure

Date	Raised by	Reference	ID #	Cluster	Description	Notes
Date the issue was identified	Who identified it	Source from which it was identified (e.g. interview notes, document ID)	Issue ID	Classification		

INFORMATION-GATHERING TECHNIQUES

Evidence comes from a variety of sources – documents, interviews, observation of the team and environment, and so on. This section discusses some of the most common information-gathering techniques.

DOCUMENT REVIEW

Most reviews probably start with documents. If we can use them to gain some understanding of the project's context and history before we meet with the project team, we need waste less of their time as we get up to speed with the project. Documents can also help us identify which areas of the project we want to focus on, who we need to talk to in each area, and what questions we want to ask them. Table 6.2 illustrates some of the purposes for document review.

Factors such as the following determine the value which can be gained from document review:

- How much documentation is the project producing? Some projects produce extensive documentation trails; some produce very little.

Table 6.2 Document review

Purpose	Useful documents
Understand project context and objectives	• Project Charter • Project Brief • Business Case • Project Inception Document
Understand project approach	• Project Plan and associated documents • Specification and design documents
Understand progress and current state of project	• Current schedule and associated items • Status reports • Risk register • Issue log • Outputs from earlier reviews • Outputs from quality assurance activities
Understand what actually happened on a project (e.g. for a retrospective)	• All the above items • Project diaries (Logs of daily events, recorded as they happen, can be useful inputs to retrospectives. The difference between people's recollection of events and the actual events can be very instructive.)

This may or may not be an issue in itself, but it certainly influences the amount of time we should put into reviewing documents.

- Why are the documents being produced? If the project is producing them merely to tick the boxes in a methodology, for example, then they may tell us little about how the project is actually being run. (However, if a lot of effort is being expended to create documents that no-one is using, that says something about the project.)

- Are the documents still current? If the project team is not maintaining them, they tell us little about the current state of the project. (Again, signs like this tell us something about the project.)

- Were the documents ever an accurate reflection of the project? Even if the documents are up to date, they are only likely to capture the generally accepted view of the project. There may be issues that people are overlooking, or that they aren't prepared to raise in documentation. (Otherwise, why would we conduct reviews?)

- How else is the project recording status and decisions? All projects have a variety of formal and informal mechanisms for recording and communicating information. We probably want to focus our attention on the mechanisms that are actually being used.

When reviewing documents, it is worthwhile considering:

- Inconsistencies within and between documents: How did they arise – is it simply that the situation changed as the documents were written, or are there more fundamental differences of perspective? How material are the differences – could different parts of the project be working from a different understanding of objectives or interfaces, for example?

- Gaps and omissions: What documents would you expect for a project of this type – are they all available? Are there aspects of the project that aren't covered in the business case and plans? Are there organizational standards or guidelines that should have been referenced? Are there risks that you'd expect to see but that aren't documented?

- Underlying rationale and assumptions: People often only record the final results of decisions. Were other options considered and why were they rejected? What assumptions underpinned these decisions? Do these assumptions still hold? Even if the authors of the documents are no longer on the project team, it may be worth talking to them to understand this rationale. Likewise, it can be worth talking to people who conducted previous reviews – even if they wrote comprehensive reports, there may be general impressions and concerns that they couldn't easily document.

- Change history: How has the document changed over time? What does this tell you about the project and external influences on it? How stable is the document now – if it's still changing rapidly, how might this affect other parts of the project?

- Comments and marginalia: What do these tell you about different perspectives and opinions within the project team? What do they tell you about how thoroughly the document has been reviewed?

Document review is a great way to improve the quality of the documents themselves (see Gilb and Graham, 1993, or Weigers, 2002). In order to assess the status and viability of a project, it provides a useful starting point, but we generally need to go to interviews to probe more deeply. Before we look at interviews, however, I want to discuss a couple of underlying skills.

LISTENING

Listening and observation are fundamental skills for reviewers. They're the main ways we gather information about the state of the project. Good listening skills help us in a number of ways.

For a start, active listening is fundamental to interviewing (which we'll discuss below). Thompson (2002) suggests that the most successful interviews are those where the interviewer talks for about 25 per cent of the time. Interviewers need to say things to keep the conversation flowing and on course, but the bulk of their time is spent listening.

Beyond that, listening adds substantial value in its own right. One of the biggest challenges for many project managers is creating time to think through their status and options. A reviewer who is prepared to sit and listen to them for a while, providing a sounding board for their thinking, can help them understand and solve their project's issues for themselves. (And project managers are more likely to implement their own solutions than those recommended by reviewers, no matter how brilliant.) As a by-product of being a sounding board, reviewers will also probably get most of the information they need to conduct an effective review.

Conversely, weak listening skills can seriously undermine a reviewer. I've seen interviews degenerate along the following lines:

Reviewer:	*Have you tried X?*
Interviewee:	*Yep – it didn't work.*
Reviewer:	*Have you tried Y?*
Interviewee:	*Yep – it didn't work.*
Reviewer:	*Have you tried Z?*
Interviewee:	*Thought about it, but it won't work for the following reasons …*

By now, the interviewee is convinced that the reviewer has nothing to offer and is wasting their time. They're much less likely to share information with this reviewer than they were at the start of the interview.

Over time, if you prove to be a good listener, people will become more comfortable about inviting your ideas and suggestions. By this time you will probably have gathered enough information to be able to make meaningful recommendations. People will listen to these recommendations because they feel you've listened to them. Until then, a reviewer's role is to listen and observe, and hence to identify what is really happening on the project.

Listening skills can't be learned from a book. However, here are some pointers to think about:

- Eliminate distractions: Wherever possible, plan to conduct meetings and interviews in a space where you won't be distracted by interruptions, ambient noise, visual clutter, and so on.

- Concentrate on what the other person is saying, not on your next question or suggestion: Focus on the facts of the situation they're describing – try to understand who was involved, when it happened and how it relates to the rest of the project, for example. If you start to think about how to 'solve' this situation, then you cease listening. Likewise if you begin to think about the next question on your checklist.

- Reflect back: Paraphrase key points and ask clarifying questions. This shows you are listening, confirms you've heard correctly, and keeps you focused on what the other person is saying.

- Prepare, but go with the flow: If you've prepared and internalized the interview protocol, as discussed below, then you'll be able to find questions that both follow from what the other person is saying and further your overall objectives. If you focus too much on a checklist of questions, then you'll keep breaking the flow of the conversation and give them the sense they're not really being listened to.

- Don't be afraid to pause: Let people catch their breath and think of the next thing to say. It often happens that someone responds to a question, then pauses to gather their thoughts, then says something significant in a second burst of information. The first response says what's at the top of their mind or what they think they should be saying. The second burst is about underlying concerns or things that are harder to express. If you ask a fresh question at the first pause, you miss this deeper information.

  (The pause probably feels longer to you than to them. Three seconds of silence while you're waiting for them to say something can seem like an eternity. From their perspective, three seconds to collect their thoughts on a complex subject feels like no time at all. Pausing to assimilate what they've said and collect your own thoughts is fine too.)

- Take notes: This demonstrates that you value what they're saying. It can also create thinking time: a couple of seconds to collect your thoughts as you finish the notes. However, don't let note taking get in the way of making eye contact and other signs that you're listening. (I find it hard to take notes on a computer for this reason: the screen and keyboard demand more attention than a pen and paper. I also find that transcribing handwritten notes gives me an opportunity to reflect on what was said. It's the beginning of my analysis.)

- Observe their body language: Tone of voice, facial expression, nervous twitches – these are all part of the message. If you don't understand them, it may be worthwhile asking: 'You grimaced then – why's that?'

- Manage your own body language: I've been interviewed by people who looked out the window as they asked questions: it didn't encourage me to give more than the barest bones of information. Make appropriate eye contact with the person you're interviewing ('appropriate' means different things in different cultures). Give non-verbal signs that you're listening: nod your head, chuckle at their jokes. When pausing to collect your thoughts, look reflective.

- Casual conversations matter too. These pointers apply to formal interviews and meetings, but also to informal encounters and corridor conversations.

OBSERVATION

Observation extends the information we gain from document review and interviews in a variety of ways. Body language gives insight into people's answers to questions. Workspaces reflect the pressures the project is experiencing. Interaction patterns illuminate the actual, as opposed to documented, governance and communication structures.

During interviews, it's worth noticing people's reactions to questions. Which ones surprise them? Do some topics make them angry, or frightened, or excited? Reading body language can be difficult, especially on multicultural projects, but questions that elicit strong responses of any kind are probably worth following up. You can at least ask why they're having that response: this may clarify the significance of their answers.

As you move through the project environment, look for signs of bottlenecks in support structures and processes: people queuing to access equipment, for example, or having trouble finding tools. Flow diagrams pinned to walls may suggest processes that are under stress. It can be worth asking someone to explain the diagram, and why they put so much effort into developing it. Cramped office space might indicate that the project team has grown well beyond the planned complement. Pizza boxes could be signs that people are working late nights. For some people, untidy desks and overflowing rubbish bins are the norm; for others they drain morale. None of these things may be problems in themselves, but they all suggest areas to explore further.

Likewise, the way the project team works together may give indicators as to how decisions are really made. Are there alliances or rivalries? Whose opinions are respected and whose are disregarded? Who is given time to talk during meetings, and who is silenced? Most teams have internal tensions.

As reviewers, we need to make a judgement as to whether these tensions are impairing effective decision making and communications. Observation alone may not answer this question, but it may suggest where to probe further.

It's also worth observing what isn't happening. What activities would you expect to happen on a project of this sort? Are people doing all the things they claim to be doing in interviews and project documentation? Are they doing things that they haven't mentioned in those sources?

Finally, are you being shielded from any areas of the project? For example, are there people it's difficult to get access to? Is this because they're overloaded, or because they have unorthodox opinions?

INTERVIEWS

Most project reviews use interviews and related meetings as their primary information gathering tool. This is because, at some level, people generally know what is happening on their project. Sometimes this knowledge is dispersed across several people and no-one has had time to integrate it. Sometimes someone can see a looming issue but doesn't fully realize its significance, or doesn't know how to articulate it effectively. By talking to people, we aim to gather their knowledge and build it into a clear picture of what is happening.

On a small review, we may do this within a single meeting. On a large review, we may undertake several dozen interviews. Either way, a similar process and skills apply. In particular, the listening and observation skills discussed above are crucial. This section looks a little more deeply at the interview process. For more detail on this subject, it is worth going to books such as Thompson (2002) or Hammersley and Atkinson (1995).

THE INTERVIEW PROCESS

Interviews can be seen as informed, structured conversations about the project. If they're well conducted, people will feel at ease and even be glad of the opportunity to structure their own thinking and convey important messages to key stakeholders. They'll be happy to provide the information that reviewers need. Conversely, if interviews are poorly managed, people will feel they're wasting their time and will give minimal information. Likewise, if we try to interrogate people, they'll resist. This just makes it harder to gather information.

Such a conversation doesn't simply happen: we need to make it happen. Table 6.3 describes eight stages for planning and conducting an interview. Naturally, the amount of effort we need to put into each stage depends on the scope of the review, but a successful interview will probably go through most of the following eight stages to some degree:

1. Planning: Identify overall objectives for the interviews, and hence plan their coverage and logistics. Begin to develop the interview protocol.

2. Interview preparation: Use document reviews, self-assessment checklists and other techniques to build a deeper understanding of the project and hence refine the interview protocol. Brief interviewees.

3. Pre-interview: Prepare for each specific interview, for example set up the room and review the objectives.

4. Opening: Set context for the interview, for example make introductions and explain objectives.

5. Mid-interview: Conduct the conversation itself, guided by the interview protocol.

6. Closing: Close and sum up. Agree next steps.

7. Post-interview: Record interview notes and other observations. Schedule follow-up activities. If interviewing in pairs or as a team, debrief with other interviewers. Confirm accuracy of the interview notes.

8. Analysis and reporting: Integrate notes across all interviews. Hence develop final analysis and reports.

This process may suggest that interviewing is complex. It is. Good interviewers bring a range of skills to bear in order to manage themselves, the environment and their interviewees. It's worthwhile seeking as many opportunities as possible to practice and develop these skills. (This is one area where dedicated review teams have an advantage over part-time reviewers: they have ample scope to practice these skills.)

Table 6.3   Interview process

Stage	Description

1. Planning	**Objectives**
	
	• Ensure that interviews focus on the overall objectives for the review, for example by asking relevant questions.
	
	• Ensure that interviews make good use of everyone's time, for example that they gather the information needed without undue need for follow-up interviews, and that logistics run smoothly.
	
	• Minimize stress on interviewers and interviewees, for example by using an appropriate environment and projecting a sense that the interviews are being conducted professionally.
	
	• Begin to establish good working relationships with interviewees and gatekeepers, and hence gain their cooperation.
	
	Activities
	
	• Define objectives for the interviews, and how these contribute to the overall objectives for the review. Objectives may be relational as well as informational: we may need to see certain people simply to establish a relationship or otherwise manage politics.
	
	• Identify coverage for the interviews – who we want to interview and how. Factors to consider here include:
	
	  – The range of people to interview (see Chapter 3).
	
	  – The order in which to interview them. (e.g. do we see the senior stakeholders first, in order to understand overall context? Are there specialist areas we'd like to cover at an early point?)
	
	  – The length of each interview. (We may only get very short slots with senior executives: how do we make the most of them? Likewise, we may only need short slots when checking facts with specialists. For other people, we may want longer sessions. However, 60 or 90 minutes is the pragmatic maximum for most interviews: beyond this, people tend to run out of energy.)
	
	  – The number of people in each interview (see 'Interviewing in Groups', below).
	
	  – Leave time to transcribe and analyse interview notes, confirm and clarify facts with interviewees, schedule follow-up interviews with people identified by the initial analysis, and so on. I find that if I try to schedule more than a dozen interviews in a three day period, I run out of time to perform these other activities effectively.
	
	• Begin to develop the interview protocol. (This defines the questions you will ask in order to achieve the interview's objectives, and how you will ask these questions. See the discussion below.)

Table 6.3   *Continued*

Stage	Description
	• Establish contact with administrators and gatekeepers. You will probably need to work with office or project administrators to book rooms, schedule interviews with project team members and arrange facilities. Access to some interviewees may also be mediated by 'gatekeepers', for example, personal assistants who control the diaries of senior executives or account managers who control access to external stakeholders. It is worth establishing good relationships with these people, for a number of reasons: – They know how to make the logistics happen in this environment. – They may be able to make it easier to access some stakeholders. – They may influence the perception of stakeholders. The way a personal assistant or account manager introduces you can do much to colour the subsequent relationship with an executive. – They may know a lot about what is really happening on the project. Most communications and gossip get channelled through these people at some point. – Beware, however, that some gatekeepers can have a negative influence. For example, they may steer you towards the people they have the best relationship with, rather than the most knowledgeable people. • Arrange logistics for the interviews. These include: – Booking rooms. Interviewing in a dedicated room gives you control over privacy and interruptions, and allows you to assemble any materials you might need – flip charts and pens, for example. Going to the interviewee's office gives you less control, but people may be more relaxed in their own space, and it provides an opportunity to observe their work environment. Each has its advantages. – Arranging room layout and furniture. You'll need a table to write on, and an appropriate number and configuration of chairs. A visible clock helps manage timekeeping. Do you want to provide coffee or water or other refreshments? What else might you need? – Arranging other facilities. Do you need special equipment for the interviews (perhaps network connections or a projector)? – It's surprising how much effort it can take to arrange these things (see Chapter 7), especially when working outside your own office environment. However, smooth logistics and a well-managed interview environment help set interviewees at ease, signalling that you are managing the process and won't waste their time. • Schedule the interviews. Again, this can take a lot of effort as you negotiate diaries. Be clear about where you can be flexible, and where you need to be firm. (e.g. you may need to see the project manager at an early point, but can be more flexible about the order in which you meet technical members of the project team.)

Table 6.3 *Continued*

Stage	Description
	• Avoid back-to-back interviews if at all possible. You'll need time to debrief one interview and collect your thoughts for the next. You may need to manage interviewees who overrun or arrive late. You will also need meal and comfort breaks.

2. Interview preparation	**Objectives**
	
	• Understand the project in order to ask relevant questions.
	
	• Ensure that interviewees are prepared for the interview so that, for example, they have relevant information to hand.
	
	• Convey professionalism, so that interviewees will be at ease and will be more likely to accept the review's findings.
	
	Activities
	• Review project overview documentation.
	• Review relevant detailed documentation.
	• Prepare and disseminate a briefing pack for the project team and other interviewees. This may cover:
	  – objectives of the review;
	  – overview of the approach being used;
	  – review schedule;
	  – objectives and agenda for individual interviews;
	  – protocols for confidentiality, following up interview results, communicating the review's outputs, and so on;
	  – anticipated outputs from the review.
	  – It's often helpful to provide the briefing pack when you book time in people's diaries, so they know what the meeting entails. However, you may not be able to finalize the briefing until all interviews are scheduled. In this case, it may be worthwhile to break the briefing into an introduction (review objectives and approach) and details (interview schedule and objectives).
	• Send self-assessment questionnaires to the project team, then assemble and analyse their responses. Factors to consider here include:
	  – Self-assessments are a good way to gather information about the project and the team's perceptions of it. They also help interviewees to prepare, for example, by alerting them to the type of information you are seeking. This means they can come to interviews ready with all the necessary information.
	  – It's unlikely that everyone will fill in a self-assessment (unless you have power to mandate its completion). Some people will appreciate the opportunity to use a self-assessment to gather their thoughts. Others won't. You may be able to encourage the latter to complete the assessment as a follow-up to the interview.

Table 6.3   *Continued*

Stage	Description
	– Long questionnaires are less likely to be completed than short ones. It may be useful to send different questionnaires to different people – overview questions to the project manager and more focused questions to technical specialists, for example.
	– Another possible strategy is to circulate the questionnaire in advance, then to complete it together at the interview. (This reduces the time available for more wide-ranging discussion during the interview.)
	– People will need time to fill in the questionnaire. However, if it is circulated too far in advance, they may forget some of the details by the time they get to their interview.
	• Confirm logistics for interviews (time, location, agenda). If people need to travel to the interview location, it may be worthwhile to assemble maps and directions. Likewise, if conducting a conference call, ensure that the dial-in details are correct and that there are no misunderstandings about time zones and such like.
	• Use the information gathered during this stage to refine the interview protocol. For example, some questions may be adequately answered by the self-assessments, while new questions come into focus.
3. Pre-interview	**Objectives**
	• Be prepared to conduct the interview. (This preparation both helps us to respond to whatever might be said during the interview, and signals to the interviewee that we respect their time and contribution.)
	Activities
	• Review objectives for this interview, and how they contribute to the overall objectives for the review.
	• Review the interviewee's role and background, and any information they provided during the Interview Preparation phase.
	• Ensure the room is tidy and arranged appropriately.
	• Ensure you have all the necessary facilities to hand (pens, paper, checklists and discussion materials, and so on).
	• Clear your mind and be alert and ready to conduct the interview.
4. Opening	**Objectives**
	• Set the interviewee at ease.
	• Establish objectives and overall direction for the interview.
	Activities
	• Interviewers introduce themselves and their roles (for the interview, for the review, and within the wider organization).

Table 6.3   *Continued*

Stage	Description

	• Describe objectives for this interview, and how these relate to the review's overall objectives. (It may be worth exploring the interviewee's reaction to these objectives: do they see the need for such a review, for example?)
	
	• Check whether the interviewee has any questions. (This helps set them at ease. Their questions may also tell us something about the project.)
	
	• Confirm logistics. How long will the interview last? How will you follow up afterwards?
	
	• Confirm note-taking and confidentiality protocols. How will you review your notes with the interviewee to confirm you've heard correctly? Are their responses confidential, or will they be shared with other people?
	
	• Ask some simple questions to set them at their ease. (e.g. how long have you been on the project? What is your role?)
	
	• Be prepared to deal with common issues, for example:
	
	   – People arrive late and flustered. You will need to set them at ease. You may also need to re-plan the interview to focus on key questions, or reschedule it.
	
	   – Problems with the room or other logistics – extraneous noise or double bookings, for example. Do you take time to find another room, or continue the interview despite the imperfections? It helps to have options up your sleeve.
	
	   – Don't be afraid to take a couple of minutes to calm down after dealing with such things. It may be better to take five minutes to have a coffee together, rather than to start the interview while you're still stressed.

5. Mid-interview	**Objectives** • Gather information **Activities** • Ask questions, as per the interview protocol (see below). • Record notes (see below). • Listen actively and observe (see above).
6. Closing	**Objectives** • Respect the interviewee's time by closing on schedule. • Confirm we've heard their main messages. • Take a final opportunity to gather information that hasn't yet been covered. • Open up the opportunity to continue the conversation, perhaps by email or other channels. • Close on a friendly note, so the interviewee conveys a positive message to their colleagues.

Table 6.3 *Continued*

Stage	Description
	Activities
	• I like to recap the main messages I've heard from the interview so far, then ask a few meta-questions, such as:
	– Is there anything else we should be asking?
	– What else would you ask if you were reviewing this project?
	– Have any of the questions we've asked surprised you?
	– Is there anyone else we should be talking to?
	• Explain how the interviewee can contact you to pass on any additional information that occurs to them.
	• Explain next steps: how you will confirm your interview notes, how findings from the review will be disseminated.
	• Thank them for their time and contribution.
	• Effective closing is very important. If the interviewee feels their time has been respected and you've listened to their contribution, they're more likely to accept and act on the findings from the review. It is better to cut the mid-interview short than to rush the closing stage. If necessary, schedule a follow-on interview to cover the remaining ground.
7. Post-interview	**Objectives**
	• Confirm and record notes from the interview.
	• Perform any follow-up activities.
	Activities
	• Debrief with other interviewers. Discuss your overall impressions and check whether they noted anything that you missed. Discuss differences and identify any activities needed to clarify them.
	• Log any artefacts (documents or other materials) received during the interview.
	• Transcribe interview notes (see the discussion on recording notes, below). It's generally best to do this as soon as possible after the interview, while it is still fresh in your mind. Some interviewees remember important points after the interview, so be prepared to integrate these into your notes also.
	• Confirm your notes with the interviewee. You will probably have two types of information within your notes: what the interviewee said, and what you observed or interpreted during the interview. It's worth checking that you heard and recorded the former accurately, and didn't miss any key points. (This may also prompt them to recall further information.) You may wish to keep observations and interpretations separate at this point.
	• Schedule any follow-up activities, for example:
	– Additional interviews to confirm or cross-check points raised by this interview.

Table 6.3   *Concluded*

Stage	Description
	– Interviews with additional people identified during this interview.
	• I generally reckon that each hour of interviewing will lead to two hours of recording and analysing notes, confirming and cross-checking facts, updating the issues log, and so on.
8. Analysis and reporting	**Objectives** • Commence analysis of information received during the interview. • Integrate this information with that from other sources. • Develop final findings and recommendations. **Activities** • Extract key points from the interview notes into the central issues log. • Consider how these points relate to those made in earlier interviews. Are trends or clusters of issues starting to emerge? Does this suggest additional questions you might want to ask, or additional people you may need to talk to? • Compare the points identified during interviews with those raised in the initial self-assessments and document reviews. How well does the project team's perception of their status align to that of the review team? • Be prepared to explore different ways of classifying and clustering issues. There is generally more than one way to cluster a set of issues: different schemes may highlight different aspects of the project. Likewise, initial impressions may need to be revised in the light of subsequent interviews. • Be aware that thinking about clusters and classification can bias your interviews: you may begin to focus on seeking information that confirms your hypotheses, and hence miss other issues. However, you will probably begin to generate hypotheses no matter what you do, so it's best to make them explicit. That way you can manage your biases and cross-check your thinking with other members of the review team. • There's a natural tendency to focus on problems as we do this. However, it's also worthwhile noting what is working well on the project: this will help gain buy-in from the project team, and may be worth disseminating to other projects. • On larger reviews, it is probably worthwhile scheduling a daily wrap-up meeting to integrate your findings and undertake this analysis. It may be worthwhile to invite members of the project leadership to this meeting. For example, they may be able to confirm the accuracy of facts and suggest additional people to interview to cross-check the analysis. Involving them in the process also helps build their buy-in to your findings and recommendations. • Reporting is discussed in more detail in Chapters 8 and 9.

THE INTERVIEW PROTOCOL

The interview protocol captures our thinking about the information we want to gather and the questions we will ask in order to gather it. Time spent developing this protocol helps us to manage our priorities during each interview. For example, it helps us to steer interviewees towards the most important areas of the project and ensures that we don't forget important topics. It also helps manage the timing of interviews: in a 60-minute interview, we probably can't cover more than a dozen major questions (with supplementary clarifying questions).

As discussed in Chapters 3 and 4, the review's Terms of Reference define the type of information we wish to gather. As we develop the interview protocol, we will combine techniques from five main classes to help us get at this information:

1.   Closed questions: These elicit a short, factual answer ('yes', '753', '3rd of March'). They are a good way to gather and validate basic facts about the project. The response is generally unambiguous, and it is easy to compare and analyse responses from multiple sources. On the other hand, closed questions don't give much scope to probe and explore.

2.   Open questions: These elicit a longer, narrative answer. For example, 'Describe how people update the configuration baseline'. Such questions can generate a lot of information about what is happening on the project. However, they can also generate a lot of noise, for example as people wander off topic. The responses require more effort to clarify and analyse than those from closed questions.

3.   Clarifying questions: These follow up an earlier answer, for example to check you've heard correctly or to clarify specific details. They often restate or paraphrase the earlier response, for example 'You mentioned that creating a configuration baseline takes too long – which parts of the process are particularly lengthy, please?' Clarifying questions may be open or closed.

      By their nature, specific clarifying questions are hard to prepare in advance. However, it's worthwhile thinking about the type of response you might get to other questions, and hence what type of follow-up questions might be needed. Useful clarification techniques include:

- Seeking other viewpoints, for example, 'How would person X describe that process?' (As well as drawing out fresh insights, this may probe people's awareness of divergences within the team.)

- Seeking the data behind opinions, for example, 'What are they doing that causes you to think they're not committed to the schedule?'

- Seeking underlying assumptions, for example, 'Under what circumstances does that process not apply?'

4.   Meta-questions: These are designed to elicit questions, either directly or indirectly. For example, 'If you had the original project manager here now, what questions would you like to ask her?' or 'Are there any questions you expected us to ask?' Such questions can be a good way to draw out areas of uncertainty and doubt. They also help capture useful questions for future interviews.

5.   Observation: It can be useful to ask people to demonstrate processes or systems. For example, 'Could you show us how you create a new baseline, please?' This may draw out issues that are so ingrained that people no longer notice them, or highlight divergences between the actual and the documented process.

Most interviews use a mix of question types. If you ask too many questions of the same type (e.g. a long succession of closed questions; or a succession of short, open questions followed by long answers from the interviewee), the interview starts to feel more like an interrogation than a conversation. A typical interview might:

- open with a meta-question ('Do you have any questions?') to set the interviewee at their ease;

- ask a couple of simple, closed questions to establish basic facts ('When did you start on the project?');

- move into a sequence of broader, open questions interspersed with open and closed clarifying questions and the occasional observation question;

- end with a couple of meta-questions.

Our position in the analysis loop may influence this mix of questions. We noted earlier that we may enter the analysis loop with some initial hypotheses, or we may begin with more open-ended data gathering. This leads to two broad schools of interviewing: directive and non-directive.

In directive interviews, we adhere closely to a checklist of questions. If discussion strays from this list, we pull it back on course by asking the next question. This works well when we are clear about the ground we want to cover, and want to ensure we cover the same ground in multiple interviews. It's a good way to gather statistical survey data, for example, or to gather the facts necessary to confirm or refute a particular hypothesis. Closed questions will predominate.

Non-directive interviews, by contrast, tend to employ more open questions, using each question as a trigger for conversation. Once the conversation has started, we use clarifying questions to maintain the interviewee's flow, letting them tell us what is important. People often have a good sense of what they're concerned about, even if they sometimes have trouble articulating it. Non-directive interviews are a good way to draw out these concerns. There is a risk that the interviewee will meander in no certain direction, so we still need to use the protocol to keep ourselves broadly within the bounds of our objectives.

In practice, most interviews fall somewhere in between these two extremes. However, reviews may well start out with relatively non-directive interviews as they explore the general state of the project, then move towards more directive interviews as they seek to clarify and confirm their hypotheses.

Three final points about the interview protocol:

- Although developing the interview protocol is an excellent way to prepare for interviews, we shouldn't let it straightjacket us once we are in the interviews themselves. For a start, what we learn in the initial interviews may cause us to revise the protocol as we proceed. More importantly, the protocol shouldn't get in the way of listening to each interviewee. If they are talking freely and giving us useful information about the project, it generally makes sense to go with the energy, occasionally nudging them back on course if necessary. I prefer to spend a lot of time developing the protocol, but don't actually take it into interviews. That way I will have internalized the questions and can focus my attention on the interviewee.

- Likewise, a good interview protocol is no substitute for basic listening and observation skills. Concentrate on what the interviewee is saying. Reflect back and clarify. Don't be afraid to allow silence and pauses so they can collect their thoughts and get a second wind.

- We noted earlier that you may need to interview some people for relational and political reasons. This doesn't mean you should abandon the protocol: use these people to give additional perspectives on the project. The worst thing you can do in a politically driven interview is appear to not take their viewpoint seriously.

WORKING TOGETHER

Some interviews are one-on-one affairs. Frequently, however, interviewers work together in pairs. Sometimes we will interview more than one person at the same time. What are the considerations here?

Interviewing in pairs allows us to divide responsibilities – typically one person takes notes while the other asks questions. This offers a number of advantages:

- The questioner can focus all their attention on the interviewee.

- The note taker can keep track of inconsistencies and areas that need clarification. (This means that the questioner needs to hand control over to the note taker occasionally, so they can ask clarifying questions. The pair needs to develop a protocol for doing this.)

- With two interviewers, we are also more likely to catch subtle nuances in the interviewee's responses and body language.

- Debriefing together at the end of the interview can bring out things that neither interviewer might have noticed separately.

The chief disadvantage is that we can cover fewer interviews than when working separately. In many cases, the increased effectiveness of our interviews outweighs this disadvantage.

Before conducting a pair interview, clarify how you will work together. Who is taking notes and who is asking questions? How will you deal with pauses and silences? Do you need to agree a signal to hand control from one interviewer to the other (when the note-taker has some clarifying questions, for example)?

Likewise, it can sometimes be useful to interview more than one person at the same time. When we have several people together, they may spark off each other – one person's observations draw additional comments from other interviewees, or differences of opinion emerge that would have been difficult to elicit in individual interviews. We may also observe interaction patterns that tell us much about how people work together on the project.

Such group interviews also allow us to cover more people in a given number of interviews. Their principle disadvantage is that they sacrifice privacy: people may be more circumspect about some topics in the presence of their peers or managers. Or the more vocal people in the group may dominate, making it difficult to elicit the opinions of quieter team members.

Workshops are used less commonly on project reviews, but they are a natural extension to group interviews. They can be a good way to drill into complex issues where you need to bring multiple perspectives to bear. They also allow us to observe interactions amongst a broad group of people on the project team. Because a workshop involves many people, it wastes a lot of time if it's not planned carefully. Likewise, running a workshop requires appropriate facilitation skills. (Retrospectives often make good use of workshops – see the case study *Post-Project Reviews and Retrospectives*.)

ELECTRONIC INTERVIEWS

Geographically dispersed projects are increasingly common. This means we often need to conduct electronic interviews – conference calls, videoconferences and online conferences. Most of the above discussion applies equally well to such interviews. There are a few additional points you may need to consider:

- We typically use facial cues and body language to manage our conversations: for example, who talks when. If these cues are absent, as on conference calls, then we need to agree protocols for identifying who should talk next, handling interruptions, and so on.

- Technical glitches can seriously reduce the effectiveness of the interview. It pays to set up the technology well in advance, and to spend some time practising with it. This is especially true for online conferences which require software to be downloaded or installed.

- Likewise, transmission delays (especially common on videoconferences) and voice quality issues (e.g. when using mobile phones or cheap Voice over Internet Protcol (VoIP) services such as

Skype) can affect the effectiveness of interviews. Again, it pays to practise with the service in advance.

- If these technical factors combine with cultural factors (strong accents, need to work in non-native language, different norms for handling interruptions), the interview can be doubly difficult. It may be better to be less ambitious with the technology (conference call rather then videoconference, say), reschedule the interview until everyone can access a landline, and send out preparatory materials well in advance.

Most of this comes down to preparation. Electronic communications need more preparation than face-to-face communications because they make it harder to deal with any problems that might arise. In many organizations, these communication modes are now the norm and hence people accommodate them well, but there are still a significant number of organizations and projects where this isn't yet the case.

RECORDING NOTES

Note taking is an important part of interviewing. The way we take notes influences the interview itself, and well-organized notes make subsequent analysis much easier. In situations where a strong evidential chain is required (especially when a project is subject to litigation), poor note taking can seriously damage the utility of our findings. As we develop the interview protocol, therefore, it's worth thinking about what notes we will take and how we'll take them.

Looking first to what notes to take, I favour taking copious notes, recording as much as possible of what I hear and observe during the interview. There are a number of reasons for this:

- It can be very hard to know what is important. What sounds like a throwaway comment in one interview can become significant in the light of subsequent interviews. So it's worth recording the comment.

- Quotes from members of the project team are often very powerful in the final report: they make issues seem more real. Extensive notes make it more likely we'll have relevant comments to back our analysis.

- Detailed notes make it easier to identify small inconsistencies within and across different people's stories. Many of these inconsistencies will be unimportant, but some of them may provide a lead into important issues. (This is especially true if people are trying to withhold information.)

- Recording selectively can reinforce biases. If we record some things and not others, interviewees may start to notice and steer their answers towards the things we record. This can mean we don't hear about certain issues.

- Taking notes can be a way to buy thinking time. As I record the information, I also gain some time to think about it and identify follow-on questions.

Of course, this increases my subsequent transcription and analysis effort, and can make it difficult to engage fully with the interviewee, but I generally find this note taking to be invaluable.

Coming to how we take notes. There are many ways to do this – within boxes on checklists, in notebooks, direct into a computer, into a tape recorder. Here are some of the factors that affect the way we take notes:

- Recording against a checklist works well when conducting directive interviews. I find it much less useful for non-directive interviews, where we rarely follow the anticipated order of questions.

- Recording electronically (tape, MP3 or otherwise) allows us to go back to the raw data to clarify exactly what was said. However, transcribing and analysing recordings entails substantial effort (far more than transcribing handwritten notes), and even then the recording won't necessarily capture body language and facial expressions. Finally, some people may be concerned or self-conscious about being recorded in this way.

- Recording notes direct to a computer reduces subsequent transcription effort. That said, I find that trying to use a keyboard and screen pulls my attention away from the interviewee.

- That brings us back to pen and paper, my preferred medium. With practice, it's possible to capture the gist of what's said during the interview as well as supporting observations and interpretations. I'd then transcribe these to electronic format as soon as possible after the interview, both to create a record that can be shared with the interviewee and review team, and because my rapidly taken notes tend to be fairly illegible. This transcribing takes time, but it helps me to reflect on what was said during the interview and hence commence my analysis.

• While taking notes, it's worth separating facts from interpretations. A common way to do this is to separate our notes into two columns. In one column, we record what people say and what we observe. In the other, we record our corresponding interpretations. For instance, that someone hesitated frequently while they described a process is a fact; our interpretation might be that they don't appear to understand the process. By separating fact from interpretation, we make it easer to confirm the former with the interviewee. We also make it easier to keep the two separate during our analysis.

One final point on note taking: if a review is legally sensitive in any way (e.g. performing a health check on a project where the client/contractor relationship has broken down; or if you suspect that illicit activity has taken place), you should take legal advice on how to record and retain your notes. They may be discoverable in any subsequent legal proceedings: failure to collect and retain them appropriately could prejudice those proceedings.

CASE STUDY

Assuring Fixed Price Implementations

SysInteg is a medium-sized systems integrator and IT consultancy. It has approximately 3,000 employees, with operations in the USA, Europe and India.

WHAT IS THE SIZE AND SHAPE OF YOUR PROJECT PORTFOLIO?

Typical projects range from perhaps $500,000 to $5 million. We work across most business sectors (government, financial services, travel, telecommunications, energy) and use a wide range of development technologies. At any given time we have more than 100 projects in progress, almost all of them fixed price.

WHAT SORT OF REVIEWS DO YOU PERFORM?

We conduct regular peer reviews throughout every project. The company's board mandates that we review every project at least once every six weeks – this is a key part of the way we manage our risk on fixed price contracts.

We also undertake gateways at key points in the project lifecycle, and do ad hoc health checks on especially critical or troubled projects. All of these assurance activities are sponsored at board level.

HOW DO YOU CONDUCT THESE REVIEWS?

For peer reviews, a team of three or four reviewers is allocated to the project at its inception. This team brings a mix of project management, technical and business skills, tailored to the work being performed by the project. All members of the team are from outside the project, but they'd typically be working within the same business unit. One member of the review team is designated as the team leader.

The review team leader works with the project manager to schedule reviews and manage the logistics of setting up meetings, teleconferences, and so on. They also decide what materials need to be distributed in advance of the reviews. The project manager is then responsible for circulating these materials to the review team about a week before the review meeting.

The review meeting itself lasts for about two to four hours, and is based on a series of standard checklists. We typically select a subset of these checklists for each review, depending on the style of development and the stage of the project. The review team walks through the checklists with the project manager and other senior members of the project team, identifying potential issues on the project. They then agree what actions need to be undertaken to address these issues. These actions are normally executed under the project manager's control, and monitored by the review team at the next review.

We also conduct a more formal gate review at the end of the design phase of each project. Experience has shown that having a clearly defined system design is critical to estimating the build phase of the project accurately, so this gate confirms that an adequate design has been created before we start building. The regular review team conducts the assessment, but they'd probably be supplemented by additional technical specialists.

A gate review takes longer than a regular review, perhaps a half or full day for the review meeting. This review meeting is preceded by a planning meeting, and often by a series of detailed technical reviews undertaken by technical specialists on the review team. Again, we use a standard checklist to guide this review.

For particularly large projects, or for projects that get into difficulties, we also conduct independent health checks. These are performed by a central team of project assurance specialists. Each health check is performed by two or three people from this team, and lasts two to four days. The frequency of these health checks is driven by the project's situation: typically we might conduct a health check on a major project every six months or so. Health checks focus on identifying and mitigating major risks and issues with the project.

The central project assurance team also monitors the overall review programme, ensuring that gateways and peer reviews are performed at the appropriate point in each project. They coordinate the peer review teams and take overall ownership of the project review processes. This team reports to the corporate board.

WHAT VALUE DO THESE REVIEWS ADD?

The company successfully delivers its portfolio of fixed price projects with an overall estimation variance of less than 15 per cent – significantly better than the industry average. This is not solely due to project reviews, but they are a key part of our process.

Beyond that, one member of each review team is normally an assistant project manager or senior developer, on the cusp of promotion. This helps expose people to other project experiences as preparation for promotion. It also helps us to build a pool of experienced reviewers.

Finally, members of the review team are often called upon to help out on their projects in cases of staff turnover. The reviews give us a pool of people who understand the project and hence are able to get up to speed relatively quickly.

WHAT CHALLENGES DO REVIEW TEAMS RUN INTO?

The peer review teams are drawn from other projects. For these people, getting time away from their main project can be a challenge. (One reason the teams contain three or four people is that this increases the chance that at least two reviewers will be available for any given review.)

Our projects also move fairly quickly. For example, the design phase may be only four or six weeks on many projects. This can make it difficult to schedule a gateway at the right point.

When it comes to health checks, they can be disruptive for the project team when they need to attend interviews and so on. Junior members of the project team, in particular, sometimes get nervous about what is going on.

WHAT CHALLENGES HAVE YOU RUN INTO IN SETTING UP THE REVIEW PROCESS?

In a dynamic environment, getting people's time allocated to participate in review teams is a constant challenge. Some managers, especially those with a background in sales rather than project delivery, have difficulty seeing the value of reviews. Likewise, getting people's compensation and other incentives aligned to the need to conduct reviews can be difficult.

Logistics Matter

CHAPTER

7

As they say in military circles: 'Amateurs talk tactics. Professionals talk logistics.' Simple things such as booking meeting rooms, coordinating diaries and getting access to document folders can consume an inordinate amount of time if they're not managed appropriately. This chapter brings together some of the things that need to be managed if a review team is to be able to devote its time to gathering and analysing information.

COMMUNICATIONS

Good communications are important to any sort of project, but they're especially important to a review – if we don't establish and maintain good relationships with the project team and other stakeholders, they won't give us the information we need, and they won't accept our findings at the end of the review. Table 7.1 outlines a possible communication plan for a health check or other substantial review. As it illustrates, key elements of our communications strategy are likely to include:

- setting Terms of Reference with the review's sponsor;

- briefing the project's leadership team on the review's objectives and approach, and hence agreeing working practices and plans;

- briefing interviewees and other stakeholders;

- providing feedback to interviewees;

- sharing ideas within the review team, typically via a daily wash-up meeting.

Table 7.1   A possible communication plan

	Stakeholder		
Information	Review sponsor	Project leadership	Interviewees
Terms of Reference			
Objectives Outputs Resources Escalation	Defined by organizational policy or agreed when review is commissioned	Described and refined at Leadership Briefing, two to six weeks before review commences	Summarized in invitation to attend an interview (sent out after Leadership Briefing)
Review plan			
Review approach		Described at Leadership Briefing	Summarized in interview briefing pack
Interview schedule Logistics		Planned at Leadership Briefing	
Ground rules			
Confidentiality Confirming data Confirming findings Interview protocol		Agreed at Leadership Briefing	Summarized in interview briefing pack
Reporting			
Status reports	Weekly checkpoint	Daily wash-up meeting	
Final report	Two weeks after review		

REVIEW SPONSOR

Chapter 3 discussed the Terms of Reference for a review. As a quick reminder, these will probably cover:

- Objectives for the review.

- Outputs: What reports are required, and by when? What level of evidence should we be seeking to back our recommendations?

- Interview coverage: What level of resource should we invest in interviews and other information gathering? Broadly who should we be talking to?

- Escalation: What should we do if we uncover major issues, or have trouble working with the project team?

- Ground rules: Are there any special ground rules, for example regarding confidentiality of interview notes and findings?

They will probably be agreed either when the review is commissioned (perhaps by organizational policy) or at a kickoff meeting with the sponsor. It generally helps to have a written record of the Terms of Reference, not least because it forces us to be clear about what we're trying to do.

PROJECT LEADERSHIP BRIEFING

A good working relationship with the project manager and other members of the project's leadership team is essential. They understand the project intimately and hence can give many pointers as to where the review team might focus its attention. They are well placed to identify appropriate people to interview and documentation to read. They can also provide logistical support, for example to book meeting rooms and schedule interviews. And, of course, they can often block reviewers' access to people and information if the relationship becomes adversarial.

For any substantial review (e.g. a health check or gate review), the review team will probably meet with this leadership team prior to the review in order to brief them on the review's objectives and approach, and to agree schedules and logistics. Table 7.2 illustrates the agenda for such a session. Depending on the size of the review, this session might last for a half or full day. For smaller reviews, much of the material might be covered by a standard briefing pack.

BRIEFING INTERVIEWEES AND OTHER STAKEHOLDERS

Being invited to attend an interview can raise a number of concerns for the interviewee. People may worry about what the review means for the project's future (and hence their own jobs). They may be nervous about being interrogated by members of the review team, who are probably considerably more experienced than they are. At the very least, they're probably very busy and hence may not be keen to take time away from their normal activities to prepare for and attend an interview.

Table 7.2   Agenda for project leadership briefing

Item	Description
1. Overview of the review process	
	Review Team Leader describes the organizational context and process for reviews:
	• Why reviews are performed
	• Who sponsors them
	• Overview of the review process
	• Tools (e.g. checklists, self-assessments and reference models)
2. Project briefing	
	Project Manager gives an overview of the project:
	• Objectives
	• Key stakeholders and their relationship/attitude to the project
	• Plan and resources
	• Solution
	• Current status
	• Risks and issues
	• Previous reviews (What reviews have happened and what did they find? Have these findings been addressed? Are there any areas the project team would like the reviewers to look at in this review?)
3. Review objectives and coverage	
	Review Team leader describes Terms of Reference and ground rules for this review, as agreed with review's sponsor. Review and project team then jointly agree:
	• Review coverage (What documents are available? Who should be interviewed?)
	• Standards and reference models (What organizational or other standards apply to this review?)
	• Focus areas (What processes, practices, workstreams, risks, and so on, should the review team focus on?)
4. Ground rules	
	Review and project team jointly agree ground rules and working practices (within the parameters set by the review sponsor), for example:
	• Communications (Will there be regular checkpoints or other meetings? What are the contact points for raising issues? For scheduling interviews, booking meeting rooms and other logistics? How will findings be communicated to the project team?)
	• Confidentiality (Are interviewee's comments attributable? Will review findings be shared with the project team? If so, when will this happen?)
	• Protocol for confirming interview notes (How will notes be checked with interviewees? When will they be available for checking, and how quickly should the interviewee return any corrections or clarifications?)
	• Overview of interview protocol and practices

Table 7.2   *Concluded*

5. Review planning
Review and project team agree schedule for the review:
• Interviews (Who to interview and when) • Logistics (Meeting rooms and other facilities; network access; access to project folders and files) • Risks (What risks might affect the review, and how will they be managed?)
6. Actions and next steps

A briefing pack, sent out as interviews are scheduled, can address many of these concerns. It can also ensure that the interviewee brings the right information and artefacts to the interview. Finally, taking time to create a clear briefing pack signals that you're managing the process professionally, and that you value people's time. This briefing pack might describe:

- Background to the review process. A brief overview of why the organization does reviews and how it selects projects for review. If interviewees understand that reviews are a normal organizational process, then they're less likely to be concerned about being singled out for special scrutiny.

- Objectives for this review.

- What outputs the review will create, and how they'll be used.

- Who will participate in the interview and how it will be conducted.

- Protocols for confidentiality, confirming interview notes, and so on.

- Any preparation required prior to the interview. For example, should a self-assessment questionnaire be completed? Should any documents or other artefacts be brought to the interview? (The briefing might also set a limit to the amount of time people should spend preparing: the review should be aiming to minimize the disruption to the project team.)

- Time and location for the interview. If necessary, this should also include maps showing how to get to the meeting room, details of any dial-in numbers for conference calls, and so on.

- How to get more information about the interview, or about the overall review process.

This information can be covered fairly succinctly – perhaps a single page email with links to additional information, or a short presentation. Another good idea is to give the briefing at one of the project's regular team meetings: you can cover many people in one session, be available to answer any questions, and begin to gauge what sort of concerns people have about the review.

If the review is likely to be contentious or sensitive in any way (perhaps cancelling the project, with consequent job cuts, is a real option), the briefing should probably be reviewed with the project leadership or review sponsor before it is sent out to interviewees.

FEEDBACK AND CONFIRMATION

It makes sense to confirm interview notes with the interviewee as soon as possible after the interview. It's easy to mishear or misunderstand: this creates a chance to put the facts right. (This isn't always down to mishearing: sometimes the interviewee wants to rephrase things once they've seen them written down. These rephrasings may point at sensitive areas on the project.)

Confirming notes may also generate additional information. Seeing the notes may prompt the interviewee to think of fresh points. Or if they have been reflecting on the interview, confirming the notes may prompt them to share these thoughts with you.

When confirming notes, we need to consider:

- Review teams are often operating within tight time constraints. It's worth setting clear timescales for interviewees to confirm notes. I'd generally agree these at the initial project leadership briefing, confirm them in the interview briefing and again at the close of the interview, and then reiterate them when I send out the notes. If anything in the notes is particularly contentious or crucial to my findings, I might also follow up with a phone call to check it.

- When confirming notes, we're checking the facts and not our interpretations. We may also choose to share our interpretations with the interviewee, but we should be clear that it's the facts we want them to check: we have to own our interpretations and recommendations. (Sharing interim interpretations with interviewees and project leadership can be complex: it may help gather feedback and build buy in, or it may lead to preliminary thoughts being spread on the rumour mill as facts. You need to make a judgement call here.)

- Every contact is an opportunity to build relationships and gather feedback. It generally helps to let people know how things are progressing and what will happen next. It's also a good idea to ask for feedback: what could you be doing better as reviewers?

DAILY WASH-UP MEETING

On larger reviews, we need some way to share information within the review team, discuss our interpretations, and start to think about our final report and recommendations. We may also want to reshape the balance of the review in light of the information that is emerging. A daily wash-up meeting is a good way to do this. This is especially useful if the review team is operating in parallel tracks, for example with specialist technical reviewers focusing on certain aspects of the project.

This meeting can also be a good way to share interim findings with the review sponsor and project leadership, and hence to gain their feedback. For example, they may be able to confirm the accuracy and relevance of findings, suggest people to talk to for additional information, and discuss options and recommendations. Keeping project leadership in the loop also helps to build their buy-in to our final report and recommendations. (It may also cause them to act prematurely or become defensive. We need to be clear that we are sharing interim thoughts, which may evolve in the light of additional information and discussion.)

The meeting can normally be fairly informal: people simply get together to describe the information and trends that they're seeing, discuss any differences of perspective and hence plan next steps for the review. If the review is operating across multiple sites, the meeting can be conducted as a conference call.

INFORMAL COMMUNICATIONS

It's easy to get locked away in a meeting room, conducting interviews and discussing interpretations within the review team. However, this can give a message to the project team that reviewers are separate and secretive. Reviewers gain by attending to informal communications also – smiling at people we pass in the corridor, using shared kitchen space to make coffee, saying hello to receptionists. For a start, we often learn a lot about the project by participating in informal conversations. At least as importantly, projecting a friendly, approachable impression makes it more likely that people will talk in formal as well as informal contexts. It also makes it more likely that they will engage with our findings.

GOING ON-SITE

Some reviews are conducted by taking the project team off-site. (This can be particularly useful when the organization wants to generate fresh thinking or break entrenched patterns of behaviour on the project. Thus it can be useful to go off-site if the review has been commissioned as a preliminary to reshaping a troubled project. Offsite retrospectives also work well.)

More often, the review is conducted on the project's site. This creates less disruption for the project team and gives the review team the opportunity to see environmental cues about the project. Project team members are also more likely to be relaxed and open in their own environment. This can create logistical challenges for the review team, however. This section looks at some of the considerations when working on-site.

ADMINISTRATIVE SUPPORT

As mentioned in Chapter 6, it is worth establishing a good relationship with local administrative staff and gatekeepers. Their help can be invaluable when booking meeting rooms, accessing the project team's diaries, finding documentation, and so on. For a major review, it can be worth attaching someone to provide administrative support to the review team.

ACCESS

Even getting to the right location can be difficult. Consider:

- Do you need a map or directions? (You may need maps for interviewees, too, if you're using interview rooms outside their normal environment.)

- Do you need security or access passes? In some environments, separate passes or keys may be needed for the campus, car parks, buildings and project space. How will you get these?

- Do you need to carry any special identification?

- What are the opening hours for buildings and other facilities? Can you arrive before reception is open, or will you need a special pass? Do you have to notify security if you're working late?

- Are there any health and safety requirements – do you need protective clothing, for example?

- Will you have access to networks, intranets and document folders?

- Will you need access to physical filing cabinets to see project documentation?

WORKING SPACE

It's possible to conduct interviews in the staff canteen, hold wash-up meetings in the hotel bar and distribute reports via a wireless access point at the airport on the way home. Possible, but it reduces your effectiveness. Having the right space sets interviewees at ease, helps you manage privacy and other concerns, and means you can focus your attention on the project. You're likely to need some combination of:

- working space for the review team;

- interview rooms;

- workshop space;

- electronic meeting facilities.

If you can specify what you need as you're setting up the review, you're much more likely to have it when you arrive on-site. Let's look at each of these in turn.

The review team will need space where it can write up notes, conduct its analysis, and hold discussions without disturbing the project team. You may need:

- desks and chairs for each member of the review team;

- power and network access points;

- telephones (mobile phones may be supplanting landlines, but landlines are useful for calling local extensions and conducting teleconferences);

- team meeting space;

- whiteboards or flip charts to capture and organize findings;

- digital projectors for briefings and presentations;

- printers and photocopiers;

- filing cabinets;

- facilities to share, store and back up notes and other files;

- access to kitchen or tea and coffee making facilities.

(Teams that travel regularly often set up equipment packs containing such items, and ship them to the relevant location in advance of the review. This can save a lot of time and hassle.)

The key decision regarding interview space is whether you meet in the interviewees' offices or have separate interview rooms. People may be more relaxed in their own space, and they'll have easy access to artefacts they may want to show you (e.g. diagrams on whiteboards and system demonstrations). You'll also get the opportunity to observe the project environment. On the other hand, taking people out of their day-to-day context may help them see things from a new angle and generate fresh insights. It can also be easier to manage privacy and interruptions in a separate room. If you do decide to use separate rooms for interviewing, these will need sufficient space to hold the interviewers and interviewees comfortably, including chairs and a table for you to write notes on.

Workshop space is more complex. If you are planning to conduct workshops, then you will need to think about the layout of the room and how people will move around it in the course of the workshop. Will you need breakout rooms, for example? There's no substitute for local knowledge here – this is a case where you should probably be working with a local contact to book the appropriate space.

Chapter 6 discussed some of the considerations for conducting electronic interviews. You may also need electronic meeting facilities if you are conducting checkpoints with the review sponsor or working as a distributed review team for any reason. In this case, consider the following factors:

- Dedicated conferencing services are generally reliable, easy to set up and available from any phone. There may be cheaper ways to set up a small conference call, but they often entail a lot of waiting around while someone sets up the phone. (VoIP services such as

Skype are usually fine for small conferences, but you need good network access: this limits their flexibility.)

- Send out dial-in numbers, access codes and meeting times well in advance. If the meeting spans time zones, be doubly clear about the timing. If people are joining internationally, make sure they have the appropriate dial-in number.

- Agree clear protocols for who will initiate the call, who will chair, how people will introduce themselves, and so on. If you are chairing, make sure you understand how the conferencing service works, and how you will manage speaking order and suchlike.

- Set up any necessary equipment in advance. This is especially important if you're using a web conferencing service. (Shared whiteboards can be great for walking through documents together.)

TIME MANAGEMENT

Reviews can be intensive activities. On major health checks and gateways, you have a few days to get up to speed with a complex project, identify any issues and begin to make recommendations. You may be working long hours and away from your normal environment. It's easy to get overwhelmed or tired and hence to miss important aspects of the project. On smaller reviews, or when performing an ongoing oversight function, you need to juggle review activities with other tasks. Either way, effective planning and time management are essential.

Factors that you should take into account when planning include:

- Allow adequate time to read documents, get up to speed with the project and prepare the interview protocol. Without this, you risk wasting your first interviews, either because you're interviewing the wrong people or because you're asking the wrong questions.

- It's hard for people to concentrate for more than 60 or 90 minutes in an interview. (For teleconferences, 30 or 45 minutes is probably the maximum.) A well-planned workshop can last longer than this, but even that will need breaks every 90 minutes or so. Planning such workshops takes a lot of time: a good rule of thumb is five hours of preparation for each hour of workshop. (I've seen workshops where the ratio was much higher than this.)

- Allow gaps between interviews. You need time to debrief one interview and prepare for the next. You also need some contingency to accommodate overruns, and time for comfort and meal breaks. (Trying to operate without meal breaks is counterproductive: if you're hungry, you won't focus on the interviewee.)

- Allow time to write up notes soon after each interview, and to integrate and analyse data across the interviews. It makes sense to do this at the end of each day: if you leave it a few days, your handwritten notes will be harder to read and the analysis won't be timely enough to inform refinement of the interview plan and protocol. Overall, my rule of thumb is that I need about two hours of writing up and analysis for every hour of interviewing.

- You might begin to finalize the analysis and write your report immediately after the interview phase, but you need to allow some time for interviewees to check notes before you complete this analysis. A good plan is often to present tentative findings soon after the interviews, then finalize these once notes have been checked. It's also wise to review the report with the review sponsor (and perhaps the project leadership team) before finalizing it.

Considering the above, it generally makes more sense to conduct four or five interviews a day and to assimilate and analyse them effectively than to try to do seven or eight in a day and never really think about the implications of people's responses. This in turn means that scheduling more than a dozen interviews over three days is unlikely to be effective. (Fortunately, as noted earlier, most of the substantive issues generally come up in the first six to 12 interviews.) It will then probably take another two or three days of review team effort to finalize and agree the report and recommendations.

We also need to set aside time for follow-on activities such as:

- conducting a retrospective or debrief of the review;

- updating checklists to reflect experience on the review;

- monitoring outcomes from the review – were the recommendations acted on, and what impact did this have?

INFORMATION MANAGEMENT

STORING NOTES

It's easy to end up with a lot of notes by the end of a review. Just as the way we take notes influences our interviews (see Chapter 6), the way we store and index these notes affects their utility for subsequent analysis. Having the right tools to hand makes this information management easier. Table 7.3 describes some of the tools you may need.

Again, if the review is legally sensitive in any way, you should take legal advice on how to record and retain all these materials. Failure to collect and retain them appropriately could prejudice any subsequent legal proceedings.

DOCUMENT MANAGEMENT

An online document management system can aid review teams in a number of ways. For example:

- securing and sharing notes;

- managing versioning of reports as multiple people work on them;

- providing access to the current version of checklists and related documents;

- managing versioning and dissemination of updates to checklists;

- running backups.

Such a system might also be extended to record and track the issues identified by reviews. Potential benefits include:

- tracking projects' actions to address these issues, and hence monitoring the benefits realized by reviews;

- linking issues to the checklist questions which identified them, thus facilitating maintenance of checklists as discussed in Chapter 5.

Table 7.3　Considerations for storing notes

Item	Media and materials	Storage requirements	Logging and indexing
Raw interview notes	Sufficient notebooks and pens for all interviews and other meetings	If project is subject to special security or other requirements, these may need lockable storage.	Note: • Participants • Location • Date and time
Interview transcripts	Laptop computer	File storage to record master version and share it with other members of the review team. Again, this needs to be secured to a level appropriate to the project. It also needs to be backed up.	As for raw interview notes, plus: • Date confirmed by interviewee (It can help to create a standard template for interview notes, with fields for this information. It's also worth tracking changes and comments made by interviewees as they confirm the notes.)
Project documentation (paper copies received from project team)		Again, may need lockable storage if the project has special security requirements. If annotating these documents, it may be worthwhile working on copies rather than the originals. This helps separate reviewers' annotations from those on the original document. It may also help when sharing notes on politically sensitive reviews.	I generally log all documents received into a separate table within the issues log (Table 6.1). The 'Reference' column in the issues log then refers to the document ID in the document log. For each document I record: • Title • Date • Version • Author • Document ID • Source (who provided the document to me)

Table 7.3   *Concluded*

Item	Media and materials	Storage requirements	Logging and indexing
Project documentation (electronic copies received from project team)		As for interview transcripts. It's worth storing original documents as read-only, either by setting the appropriate flags or by copying them to write-once media. This prevents accidental changes to documents as you review them.	As for paper documents. (It's possible to record additional attributes for electronic documents, for example, creation and last modification date.)
Analysis of interview notes and other information	It's often useful to have a set of pens (dry wipe and flip chart), Post-it® notes and suchlike available, to support such analysis.	Digital camera to record whiteboards and flip charts, and hence save images to the file storage.	
Workshops	If I'm facilitating workshops, I bring a full workshop kit of pens, post-its, clock for timekeeping, etc		

Programme Reviews in a Merged Environment

Start-up or emerging organizations, whether private or government, have their own particular problems. For large start-ups resulting from mergers or acquisitions, developing a common corporate culture can be critical to success.

Start-ups by their nature are chaotic – they lack shared infrastructure, including basic business systems, processes and historical perspective. As staff arrive, they bring assumptions gained from working in different environments. Melding these elements into a functioning organization requires time, vision and a great tolerance for ambiguity.

If the resulting organization is not projectized – that is, it is functional in nature – programmes are likely to experience additional difficulties related to dysfunctional information flow. Programme reviews by experienced staff then become essential, both to uncover problems and risks early and to instil the beginnings of a project culture.

AN UNSUCCESSFUL MERGER

In the 1990s, Corporation X, based in the American Southwest, acquired a small telecommunications company based on the East Coast, to form the core of a new unit within a larger business unit. The parent corporation's core business was data processing, but it was emerging as a leader in client–server computing and wanted to move into the telecommunications market. Several years before this acquisition, Corporation X had itself been acquired by a much larger firm. That acquisition had been difficult, merging a union-based giant with the smaller, professionally based Corporation X.

The head of Corporation X's business unit called for a review of a mid-sized information-technology project in the acquired organization to find out both why projects in general were not successful and why there appeared to be resistance to Corporation X's project lifecycle. The review team of two began with a pre-distributed health check form that approached the project from two dimensions: the project lifecycle (initiation through close-down) and the eight areas of project management, as defined by the Project Management Institute at that time.[1] All staff, from the President to the project team, participated. The results were interesting: there was little variation in the answers – not what one would expect unless communication was excellent and the vision shared.

The review team then interviewed selected individuals onsite – representatives from the project team, the President, the two Vice Presidents, and project leaders. When the review team arrived, they noticed something unusual: although the merger had occurred almost a year before, the floors of the building were stark – none of the normal branding mandated by Corporation X. Cubes were old and small, and the floors were unusually quiet. The team planned approximately two weeks of interviews, another two weeks of analysis, and a week to brief both the project and the executives. The interview structure was similar to the health check, although the questions were open-ended and probing. The average interview lasted approximately one hour; both members were always in attendance to ensure adequate understanding of the interviewees.

As the interviews progressed, themes emerged: a feeling of isolation from Corporation X, resistance to the project lifecycle, general disorganization, low morale and little adherence to any standards. What had seemed lock-step in the health checks now appeared to be the opposite, and the review team soon realized that the teams had taken the Checks together so that answers were the same. More revealing were the interviews with the President and two Vice Presidents. The President, who had welcomed the team openly, was theoretical, philosophical, and divorced from day-to-day management of the organization. The two Vice Presidents were in open competition for control – and the eventual promotion. One, who had been brought in prior to the merger by the President to provide strategic guidance and assistance with marketing, was bitter and unhappy; the other, a long-term employee, was openly hostile to the reviewers. Neither had checked on the progress of the project; both had taken the word of the project leaders and assumed that everything was going well.

---

1   PMI's original eight areas were Time Management, Cost Management, Human Resources Management, Procurement Management, Scope Management, Risk Management, Communication Management and Quality Management.

The review's recommendations had to encompass not only a get-well plan for the project, but also a plan for institutionalizing the project lifecycle and an overall change-management plan to bring the organization into the fold of Company X's culture. The briefing to the two Vice Presidents met with a dismissive attitude. The briefing to the President, which was pointed and multi-faceted, met with surprise and confusion. He had no idea that his Vice Presidents were openly combative, that his teams were disorganized and that morale was low. He had assumed that the merger had brought in standards and a culture but had never bothered to check.

The briefing to the project team, despite the presence of the Vice Presidents, led to open discussion. Team members appeared to feel relief that Corporation X had decided to offer assistance. The review team reported back to the head of the business unit and to senior executives that the merger had in essence failed, that strong measures were needed soon, that there was a need to re-examine merger strategy in general, and that there should be on-site mentors from corporate headquarters until there was movement forward.

THE OUTCOME

There is an adage that it is wrong to introduce anything new in a troubled project. However, when major change is necessary to sustain the project and its teams, action can be justified. In this case, Corporation X removed the President, brought in a human-resources team and augmented the project team with more seasoned engineers. Six months later, there was more stability and less resistance, but within a year, Corporation X chose to disband the acquired organization and to incorporate the staff into other projects. The original project limped to a finish, and the product was assumed into Corporation X's larger offering.

LESSONS LEARNED

This review was the first of what eventually became an accepted approach to programme and project reviews in Corporation X. The review organization grew to a multi-disciplinary team of 70, with numerous engagements. The strongest lessons, however, were in the need for strong interpersonal skills in the reviewers and in the need for a greater understanding of change management and the effects of corporate culture on mergers and acquisitions. Had the initial reviewers relied only on technical expertise in telecommunications and project management, they would have missed what was ultimately the most important result of the review: bringing stability and a shared culture to the merged organization.

Training for all future reviewers included the following, in addition to education in project lifecycles:

- managing change;
- influencing change, including understanding of project and organization milieu and dynamics;
- interviewing skills;
- the original Capability Maturity Model approach, adapted to project maturity.[2]

Judith Lane, PMP

ACKNOWLEDGEMENTS

Judith Lane, PMP, is a Senior Principal Information Systems Engineer with The MITRE Corporation, a Federally Funding Research and Development Center, in McLean, Virginia, USA. The work described in this case study predates her position with MITRE.

---

2   The Capability Maturity Model (CMM) of the Software Engineering Institute has gone through numerous permutations since its first release but still remains the standard for maturing an organization in the management of IT projects.

PART III
Reviews and Governance

Project reviews help ground people in reality. In many cases it's sufficient for reviewers simply to provide a sounding board for the project team, creating space for them to think through their situation and hence address any issues. In other cases, the insight and experience provided by reviewers is all that's needed for the project team to deal with the issues.

Sometimes, however, this isn't enough. Perhaps the root cause for a project's problems lies outside the team's direct control. Perhaps the project lacks the resources to deal with a particular issue. Perhaps the issue can't be dealt with – a risk has materialized that simply can't be managed. Perhaps the project team is too close to their chosen plan and approach, and cannot see the issue even with the reviewers' perspective.

In these cases, the second barrier to performing effective reviews, described in Chapter 2, may get in the way: it can be difficult to get people to act on the findings from a review.

The recommended action may range from a minor tweak to the project's approach to a major intervention (perhaps resetting objectives or even cancelling the project). It may lie outside the project itself – adjusting the plans of stakeholders who are relying on outputs from this project, for example. Looking at the case studies:

- In *Earthquakes in the Project Portfolio*, the CFO used the information from project reviews to adjust his financial projections. Other executives used the information to shift resources between projects.

- *Weeding the Project Portfolio* discusses the difficulties of persuading project sponsors to reframe or cancel their projects.

- In *Programme Reviews in a Merged Environment*, a project review triggered senior executives to make major changes within a business unit.

In each case, reviews led to actions by the project sponsor (to provide resources or agree changes to the project charter) or other stakeholders (to adjust their plans to accommodate changes to this project).

This section looks a little more closely at what review teams need to understand in order to deliver information that people can act on. Chapter 6 discussed this question in the context of gathering evidence – how do we gather sufficient information for people to understand what we're saying and accept the need for action? However, action also requires power. If a review delivers recommendations that no-one has the power to act on, then it's wasted its time.

To conduct an effective review, we need to understand what I call the 'sphere of influence' of our review sponsor and the other stakeholders we're reporting to. Only then can we ensure that we address issues and make recommendations that are within their remit.

Chapter 8 sets out a simple model for mapping spheres of influence. I call it a 'governance matrix' because it's about understanding what decisions people can make. (My preferred definition of governance comes from the Institute on Governance (IOG): 'Governance is the process whereby societies or organizations make decisions, determine whom they involve and how they render account' (IOG, n.d.) The matrix provides a simple model to help me think about who is accountable for which decisions, and hence what sort of information I need to give them.

Chapter 9 extends the discussion to look at how project and programme governance might align to other elements of organizational governance. Organizational governance is a large subject and I don't profess to be able to cover it all. As a reviewer, however, I need to know enough about it to deal with the gaps and overlaps I come across in the course of looking at projects. (Being temporary endeavours, projects often seem to run into such gaps and overlaps: most organizations build their authority structures to deal with 'business as usual' activities.)

Of course, one aspect of triggering action is to give our review teams effective sponsorship. If they report to an executive who is committed to acting on their findings, they are much more likely to add value. We will come back to this question in Chapter 10. Chapters 8 and 9 look at the actions the review team needs to take for itself in order to maximize its effectiveness.

Triggering Effective Action

CHAPTER 8

Reviews are a trigger for action. We frame our findings so that people can intervene to run their projects and the surrounding activities more effectively. If we've done our job, then by the end of the review we will have gathered the information necessary to answer the three needs of Chapter 6:

- Understanding: People will have enough information to understand what we're saying about the project.

- Acceptance: People will have enough information to believe what we're saying.

- Action: People will know what action could be taken to address the issues.

However, none of this is of any value if people don't have the authority or ability to take the recommended actions. As we frame our findings, we need to understand the type of actions our stakeholders can take. This means understanding what I call the 'sphere of influence' of our review sponsor and the other stakeholders we're reporting to. We can then ensure that our review addresses the issues which are within their remit. For example:

- If we are reporting to senior executives who are interested in the overall status of the project portfolio, there is little point in recommending detailed changes to the structure of an individual project. They have delegated this authority to other managers. Our report needs to focus on actions relating to the shape of the portfolio. (e.g. in *Earthquakes in the Project Portfolio*, the Chief Financial Officer was interested primarily in information to inform corporate financial projections. Likewise, the Marketing Director wanted to know when to commit to major advertising campaigns. Neither wanted to hear about ways to accelerate individual projects – that was for other people.)

- If we are reporting to the project manager, there may be little point in recommending that they add resources or cancel the project: in many organizations, this will be outside their authority. Here, our recommendations need to focus on ways to use the available resources more effectively, and on how to escalate larger issues with their sponsor.

- If we are reporting to the project sponsor, then adding resources or cancelling the project may well be within their remit. Our report should focus on strategic concerns affecting the project and its relationship to other projects and overall organizational objectives. Details of the project processes and suchlike are for the project manager.

In each case, we need to frame our findings differently and so need to focus the review on gathering different information. (In many cases it will just be a matter of writing reports with different levels of detail for each stakeholder. However, the different situations may also call for differences to the way we escalate issues, to the timing of our reports to each stakeholder, and so on. Being alert to these nuances can be critical to getting our findings heard and acted on, at least in some organizations.)

This chapter gives a simple model to help understand the 'sphere of influence' of our audience. By considering this as I'm setting up a review, I find that I am better able to understand the dynamics (and politics) within and around project teams, programme management offices, project support offices, enterprise architecture teams and other stakeholders. This in turn helps me to identify who is best able to act on specific issues and how to frame my findings so they can take this action.

SPHERE OF INFLUENCE

GOVERNANCE AND DECISION MAKING

The question of who has authority to take what action is about governance. The IOG defines governance as follows:

> Governance is the process whereby societies or organizations make decisions, determine who they involve and how they render account.
> (IOG, n.d.)

Governance defines who is allowed to make which decisions, what constitutes 'due process' for making those decisions (e.g. who needs to be consulted), and how we ensure this process is followed. Review and assurance functions support good governance by ensuring that decision makers have accurate information and understand their options. (Auditors support good governance primarily by checking that the correct process is followed.)

It's also useful to be clear about what governance isn't. Governance isn't management – it defines who manages what, then lets those people get on with the job. It's also about a lot more than compliance. Compliance is the backward-looking part of governance that helps demonstrate that decisions were taken in accordance with regulations, policies and objectives. The forward-looking part of governance creates structures to help people make good decisions. Those good decisions are what add real value to the organization.

Review and assurance functions are one of those forward-looking structures. We need to frame our findings so they inform the decisions that the people we're reporting to can make.

PROJECT GOVERNANCE

Project governance is generally fairly well understood. Models such as PRINCE2 (OGC, 2005), MSP (OGC 2004a) and the various project management bodies of knowledge (APM, 2006; PMI, 2004) do much to define the key decision-making roles within the contained scope boundaries of a project or programme. Figure 8.1 (based on the PRINCE2 model; see OCG, 2005) illustrates the commonly accepted model for project governance.

Figure 8.1 shows the following roles:

- Organizational Management makes decisions about the shape of the organization's portfolio of projects, for example deciding which projects to invest in.

- The Project Board makes decisions about the overall direction of the project, and about how it will use its resources to achieve the objectives agreed by Organizational Management when they initiated the project. It generally manages by exception, setting overall direction for the Project Manager then monitoring progress, only intervening when key decisions are needed. The Project Board includes the Executive (Sponsor), who is accountable for success

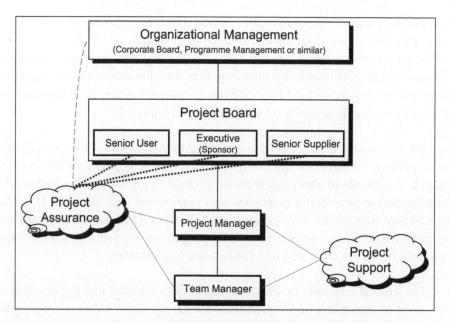

Figure 8.1   Typical project governance structures (after PRINCE2)

of the project, and senior users and suppliers, who represent the interests of those stakeholders.

- The Project Manager runs the project on a day-to-day basis on behalf of the Project Board, with all the decisions about resource allocation, planning, quality management, communications, and so on, that that entails.

- Team managers and other people on the project make decisions about how to create the products required of the project. (It's easy to overlook just how many decisions the typical member of a project team makes in the course of their daily work. Decision making is not the sole prerogative of executives.)

- Project Assurance undertakes independent monitoring of the project's progress and outputs on behalf of the Project Board.

- Project Support assists the Project Manager and team by providing administrative help and related functions.

The first four of these roles reflect the fact that four types of decision making matter to a project. Review and assurance teams can support this decision making in the following ways:

1.   External executives control the organization's portfolio of projects. Review and assurance teams give these executives a clear view of project status and alignment, so that they can manage strategic dependencies and allocate resources across the portfolio.

2.   Project sponsors make strategic decisions about objectives and resource allocation within the project. Review and assurance teams help them understand what is going on within the project, and hence when and how to intervene.

3.   Project managers make decisions about day-to-day project execution. Review and assurance teams help them maintain perspective – not losing sight of the bigger picture and not overlooking key details. This, in turn, helps them to identify problems and nip them in the bud.

4.   Project team members make hundreds of decisions every day as they create products and coordinate their activities. Again, independent review and assurance teams help them to maintain perspective and adopt good practice as they make these decisions.

Of course, the exact structure adopted by any particular project depends on the organization, project scope, and so on. Large projects in highly regulated industries, for example, will have more layers and greater separation of powers within any layer. However, most organizations will recognize some variant of this general model.

THE GOVERNANCE MATRIX

As a reviewer, I run into some practical difficulties when I try to use the above model. Although it represents decision making within most projects reasonably well, things often get fuzzier at the boundaries.

For a start, the model sees assurance as a responsibility of the project board, and hence anticipates that reviewers will report to this board. In practice, I often find myself being asked to support several, or even all, of the four decision-making roles. It's difficult to serve many masters. For example, if I'm reporting to the project manager, they naturally want to hear about any issues I identify, and be given a chance to address these issues before the project sponsor or external executives are told. On the other hand, sponsors and external executives want to know about certain types of issue as quickly as possible. I could use a model that helps me clarify the primary reporting lines and timings for different types of information.

Second, there are often managers and executives outside the project and not directly represented on the project board who nonetheless have some sort of interest in the status of a project. This may, for example, be because they have indirect dependencies on the project's outputs, or because the likelihood of its success influences decisions they must make, or because they have an interest in resources it's consuming. These people also need information about the project, and support to understand the implications of this information for their own decision making. Where do these people fit into the overall governance picture?

Finally, there are often other people who seem to think they have the right to tell a project manager what to do. Project management offices (PMOs) mandate processes and practices they must use. Enterprise Architecture Offices dictate aspects of the solution. Resource pool managers control the availability of key people. As a reviewer, I need to understand how such groups influence the project, and what information they need about it in order to perform their roles. For example, resource pool managers have a legitimate reason for wanting to know about potential delays so they can plan the availability of their people across multiple projects.

The 'standard' project governance model assumes that the project is a relatively contained endeavour, impervious to these influences, or else that all external influences are managed through the Organizational Management layer. Many organizations see a lot more horizontal information flow than this – politicking and horse trading between project sponsors, for example. When the project boundaries are more porous, how do I understand who has a stake in which information?

The net result is that I've found I need a simple model to help me position all these different groups and relationships so I can understand what decisions they're interested in and hence what information they need. (As a by product, it turns out that this model also helps me to identify who's around the project, and hence who I may need to interview. I discuss this in the next section.) To develop the model, I consider two dimensions for decision making: the type of decision involved, and the strategic scope of the decision:

1.   Type of decision: Many organizations find it useful to separate ends from means. Thus, decisions about objectives (the 'what') are separated from decisions about strategy ('how' the objectives will be achieved). Audit and assurance, confirming that the strategy is

being followed in practice and is achieving the desired results, are separate concerns again.

2.   Strategic scope of decision: This ranges from strategic, executive-level decisions to the hundreds of small decisions that junior staff make every day.

Figure 8.2 shows the resultant model. It divides each dimension into three classes. For type of decision (the horizontal axis) there is:

- Setting direction: These are the 'what' decisions, defining objectives and setting policies and standards that will have general applicability across the organization or unit.

- Implementing: These are the 'how' decisions, defining how the objectives will be achieved or the policies will be implemented within the scope of any given organizational unit or project.

- Assuring: These are the decisions we make about whether we are on course. Are we doing what we originally set out to do? If not, what might we do to get back on course?

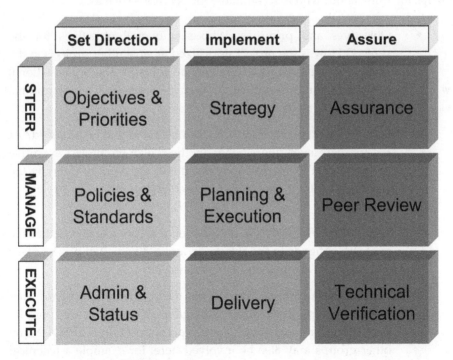

Figure 8.2   The governance matrix

Likewise, for strategic scope of decision (the vertical axis) there is:

- Steering: Setting objectives and priorities; marshalling overall budgets and resources.

- Managing: Allocating resources to achieve these priorities, and hence planning and coordinating activities, managing risks and issues, and so on.

- Executing: Performing the day-to-day activities involved with designing and building products and deliverables.

(Of course, the strategic scope of decisions can range widely: from billion dollar mergers and acquisitions to purchasing paperclips. However, these three levels suffice for most situations on a single review. For very large programmes, it may help to consider nested versions of the matrix, as illustrated later in Figure 9.1 (page 207). Managing-level decisions for the overall programme then become steering-level decisions for individual projects, and so on.)

Each of the nine cells in this matrix captures the units and activities involved in making decisions of a given type and strategic scope. Thus for a given project, it helps me think about who is accountable for decisions such as:

- Objectives and priorities: Who sets overall objectives for the project? How is the project prioritized against other projects in the portfolio? Typically, this role will be filled by the organizational board or some sort of portfolio management office or programme management team.

- Strategy: Who determines how the objectives will be achieved? At the strategic level, this is generally the role of the project executive or sponsor. (The sponsor may not do all the work of defining the strategy, but they are ultimately accountable for what strategy is chosen.)

- Assurance: Who provides an independent view as to whether the strategy is aligned to the objectives, and as to whether project plans and activities are aligned to the strategy?

- Policies and standards: Who defines the policies and standards that apply to the project? Project management standards are typically owned by some sort of PMO or project support office (PSO). Many other groups may also be involved here, for example a technical design authority may define technical standards or a security team may set security policy and standards. (This cell identifies the source for many of the reference models we use as we perform reviews.)

- Planning and execution: Who defines the detailed plans for delivering the strategy? Who coordinates people and resources to execute these plans? (This person, typically the project manager, is responsible for combining the objectives and strategy coming from above with the policies and standards coming from the left in order to develop a feasible project plan.)

- Peer review: Who undertakes assurance at the more day-to-day level, for example confirming that individual tasks and products align to the project plan? (I have called this cell 'Peer review', by comparison to 'Assurance' in the cell above, as peer reviewers often undertake this more tactical role. Some organizations may operate differently.)

- Admin and status: Who defines and supports tools and templates for tracking project status and other administrative information? This is typically the role of the PSO, if one exists.

- Delivery: Who are the poor Indians surrounded by the Chiefs in all the other cells?

- Technical verification: Who is responsible for independent quality assurance and similar tasks?

The people undertaking these decisions or actions require different types of information. They are also likely to have different levels of technical and project management expertise, so may need this information to be presented in different ways. By understanding who these people are and how they relate to each other, I am better able to deliver the information they need in a format they can understand. (I am also able to identify potential gaps and overlaps in the organization's or project's decision making: often a useful outcome from a review.)

Governance is a complex subject. This matrix doesn't cover every situation, but it does give me a simple model I can carry in my mind and use to explore the roles, relationships and information needs of some key stakeholders. It doesn't replace the PRINCE2 model of project governance, or any other model: it complements them, giving me a slightly different perspective on who's likely to be involved in decision making on the projects I'm reviewing.

IMPLICATIONS OF THE GOVERNANCE MATRIX

PROJECT GOVERNANCE ROLES

The four decision-making roles described by project governance models fill four of the cells in the governance matrix: 'Objectives and priorities', 'Strategy', 'Planning and execution', and 'Delivery', as illustrated in Figure 8.3. The matrix is often useful for asking questions about how these roles relate to units in the other cells, such as PMOs, PSOs and project assurance teams.

PEER REVIEW AND INDEPENDENT ASSURANCE

Review and assurance teams may operate at any of the three levels of strategic scope in the matrix. Our primary reporting line typically determines the level we are operating at: if we are reporting to the project sponsor, project board or an external executive, then we are probably operating at the 'Assurance' level. If we are reporting to the project manager, then we are likely to be undertaking peer review. Figures 8.4 and 8.5 illustrate these reporting lines. They also illustrate a typical communication pattern: review and assurance teams gather information from people below and to the left of them, in order to report to people at the same level.

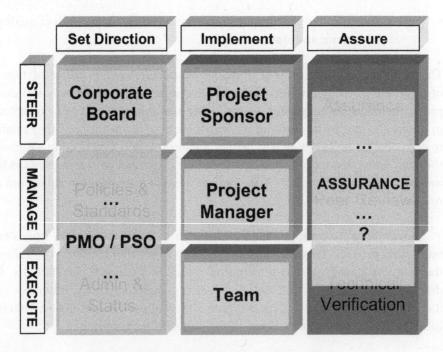

Figure 8.3   Project governance and the governance matrix

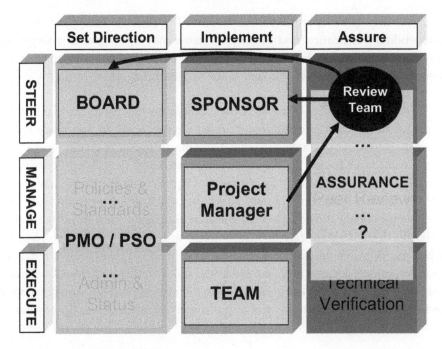

Figure 8.4   Independent assurance

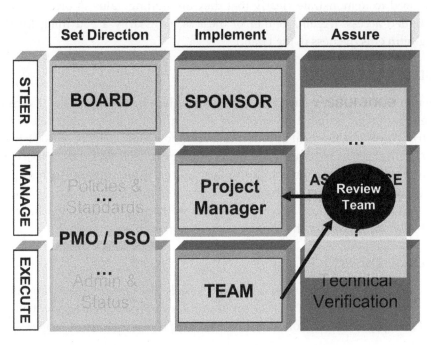

Figure 8.5   Peer review

Assurance teams operating at the 'Execute' level are less common (although Independent Verification and Validation teams may operate at this level). As noted below, I believe that one of the reasons agile development approaches succeed is that they actively address assurance at this level.

The level at which we report often influences the protocols we use for accessing people and information. At one extreme, audit or assurance teams who report to the corporate board may have the authority to go anywhere they please and to talk to anyone they like. (The case study *Completion Bonds in the Film Industry* describes another situation where assurance teams have such authority.) Such a team might even interpret denial of access to indicate that a problem is being hidden. (Just because an assurance team has this level of authority doesn't mean they should exercise it. It usually makes more sense to build good working relationships than to gain access by executive fiat. And once you do call for executive backing, you risk creating a stand-off whereby you will need it for all future access. This in turn risks alienating your executive backers – they may eventually tire of putting effort into backing the assurance team.)

At the other extreme, peer reviewers reporting to the project manager may need to negotiate carefully to gain access to some stakeholders. They may also need to demonstrate clearly that they are adding value in order to earn continued access. (Again, neither of these is necessarily a bad thing for the long-term effectiveness of the team.)

AGILE DEVELOPMENT

We noted above that assurance teams operate less frequently at the 'Execute' level of strategic scope. This often leaves a gap in the lower right cell of the matrix. Agile development approaches (see, for example, Schwaber, 2003; Beck and Andres, 2004; Derby and Larsen, 2006; Johnson, 2006; Richards, 2007), with their emphasis on openness and visibility and use of techniques such as pair programming and agile coaching, do much to populate this cell. This makes it harder for people to lose touch with reality in their daily work, and hence is probably one reason for the success of these approaches.

ROLE OF THE PMO

The role of the PMO is often confusing, largely because people mean many things by 'PMO'. Whether project, programme, or portfolio management office, the PMO has a different role at each of the three levels of strategic scope:

- At the steering level, a PMO influences the prioritization of projects and the allocation of resources across the portfolio.

- At the management level, a PMO owns project management processes and standards for the organization.

- At execution level, a PMO (or PSO) will tend to control mechanisms for reporting project status, tools to support project management processes and suchlike.

Unfortunately, the name of the unit doesn't always indicate which level it is operating at. If 'PMO' translates to programme or portfolio management office, then it may well operate at steering level, but equally it may operate at management level. A project management office is more likely to operate at management level, but may extend into either steering or execution roles. A PSO generally operates at execution level, but again may have broader strategic scope in some organizations.

The governance matrix provides a tool to explore this question and determine just what level the PMO operates at. This helps explain which reference models it controls, what influence it has over project prioritization and resource allocation, and so on. This in turn determines the type of information it needs and the type of issues that should be escalated to it.

THE SPONSORSHIP FORK

Project sponsors have a difficult role. Their position at the middle of the top row of the matrix means that they provide a bridge between steering and implementation functions, and between the project team and the wider organization. This can require them to operate in two domains, each with their own jargon and mindsets. Few sponsors are equally at home in both domains, leading to two common dynamics:

- Sponsors micro-manage the project. In effect, the sponsor takes on the project management role. This diverts them from their proper role of managing external stakeholders, setting priorities and removing external barriers to the project. It can also de-motivate the project manager and other members of the project team.

- Sponsors stand back too far from the project, leaving the project manager to set strategy and manage all stakeholders. To the extent that this reflects confidence in the project manager, it can be a good thing. However, it often leaves the project manager trying to resolve issues, for example of organizational priorities and resource conflicts, that they are ill-placed to address.

Both dynamics indicate that the sponsor lacks either the information or the understanding they need to take effective action to support the project. Strong project managers can manage their sponsors, helping them understand what support they must provide. Where this is not happening (perhaps because the project manager is fully loaded managing a complex project; perhaps because the sponsor is unable to admit that they don't fully understand the project and their role to support it), reviewers can do much to help sponsors understand the status of the project, and to mentor them as to when and how to intervene.

ASSURANCE AS AN INFORMATION CONDUIT

The 'sponsorship fork' is one dynamic whereby weak communication can damage a project. Reviewers can do much to address weak communications within and around the project.

For example, project teams often have problems communicating messages about risks and issues to project sponsors or external executives. They may lack the knowledge and political savvy to frame such messages appropriately. They may lack access to the executives who can act on these messages. Or they may lack the credibility necessary for the messages to be heard when they are delivered. In such cases, project reviewers can help the team frame the message and deliver it to the appropriate stakeholder. Likewise, project sponsors and external executives often have trouble picking out the critical information from the multitude of messages that come their way. Assurance teams can help them to prioritize the messages and hence to frame appropriate interventions.

The governance matrix helps us identify which communication paths we want reviewers to focus on. Should they focus on improving communications between the project manager and sponsor, ensuring that they understand what is happening and hence can communicate it more widely? Or is their primary role to ensure information gets to key external stakeholders, with any support for the project manager and sponsor being a by-product?

Either of these approaches can be useful. However, if reviewers are focusing on communication between the project and external stakeholders, then they need to manage the risk that they undermine communication within the project. Some organizations, for example, set up a review process because they are not getting the information they need from their project managers. If this original failure was due to the project managers' weak communication skills, the review process may simply embed those weaknesses: project managers are never given the opportunity to improve. In such cases, reviews may address the immediate problem, but the organization will probably gain most benefit if reviewers also address the root cause by mentoring project managers in their communication skills.

TIMING OF REVIEWS

The frequency and timing of reviews is often influenced by the layer at which reviewers are operating. At the 'Execute' layer, reviews are generally framed to provide rapid feedback to project team members so that they can adjust their actions in 'real time'. In this case, it makes sense to conduct small, frequent reviews.

At the 'Steering' layer, larger and less frequent reviews may be more useful. This layer is epitomized by gate reviews: executives are interested in a small number of major decisions at key points in the project lifecycle. Reviews are framed to provide input to these decisions.

INTERVIEW COVERAGE

Finally, the governance matrix provides a useful check on our interview coverage during reviews. To get a rounded view of the project, its decision making, and its alignment to the wider organization, we might expect to talk to someone in each of the cells.

WRITING REPORTS

Understanding our audience and their information needs is key to framing effective findings and recommendations. However, there are a number of other things to consider when we prepare our final report and other outputs. This section discusses five such factors:

1.   separating fact from interpretation;

2.   building a clear chain of reasoning;

3.   language and style;

4.   engaging in dialogue;

5.   building credibility.

SEPARATING FACT FROM INTERPRETATION

When writing reports, I find it useful to maintain a clear separation between facts, interpretations and recommendations. In many cases, simply documenting the evidence gathered from our interviews and observations is enough to give people a clear picture of what is happening on the project and hence what they need to do to improve things. This evidence also provides solid grounding for discussion of the issues and their root causes, and hence for recommendations on how to address them. Without such grounding, it's easy for people to dismiss or dispute our findings.

I find the Satir Interaction Model (Weinberg, 1994) to be a useful framework for structuring my thinking here. It organizes communications into four phases:

- Intake: What have we seen or heard during the review? The focus here is on specific, objective information. Ideally, it will have been verified from several sources. This information provides the factual base from which we build our findings.

- Meaning: What do we interpret this information to mean? Does it suggest that certain processes are not working, for example, or that people are overlooking particular issues? What might be the root causes for these issues?

- Significance: What impact are these issues likely to have? Do they threaten the project's objectives, or are they damaging people's productivity and efficiency? Or do they simply represent an inconvenience that can be lived with? (It's also worthwhile identifying things with a positive impact: things that the project is doing especially well. This helps people to hear our other findings, and may be worth disseminating to other projects.)

- Response: What could be done to address these issues and root causes? If there are multiple options, what are the strengths and weaknesses of each option? Which option do you recommend, and why? The more specific the recommendations, the better: ideally, we should identify who is responsible for actions, when they should be performed by, and how we will recognize that they have been performed effectively.

The degree of detail with which we report this information will vary. Some audiences may prefer an executive summary, while others want to see detailed evidence with full traceability onto our recommendations. As we build credibility, people may be happy simply to receive recommendations without any supporting detail. Even in such cases, having the full chain clear in our minds helps us to be confident of our ground. It also makes it easier to re-examine our interpretations as new information comes in.

There is also a fifth stage in this chain – feedback. It's worth asking the review sponsor and other recipients for feedback on our reports. Do they give the information they need? Is there anything that's surprised them, either in what we've said or in what we haven't said? This may signal other things we need to consider, either for this review or as we frame future reports.

BUILDING A CLEAR CHAIN OF REASONING

It's easy to leap to interpretations and recommendations that are weakly or incorrectly linked to the underlying evidence, especially when under time or political pressure. As we develop the above chain from facts to recommendations, it's important to test the linkages and ensure that they're well founded. Do our interpretations really explain the facts? Are there other interpretations that could explain them equally well? Will our recommendations address all the issues?

This is especially important if our findings are likely to be contentious or to run into resistance. It can also be important if the issues and recommendations seem obvious from the outset: review teams sometimes focus on their initial thoughts and fail to take in new information during the course of the review, slipping into a type of 'groupthink'. One way to avoid such groupthink is to ask someone to consciously act as a 'devil's advocate', constantly probing conclusions and looking for weak points in the chain of reasoning.

LANGUAGE AND STYLE

We should be aiming to write as clearly and simply as possible. Extraneous information or complexity simply distracts from the core findings. The results from most reviews can be summarized into a relatively short report. (e.g. the reviews described in *Formal Gateways in the Public Sector* are substantial pieces of work, but their findings are summarized into six to 12 pages.) If necessary, detailed evidence can be consigned to appendices.

At the same time, every organization has its own conventions and templates for writing reports. We should respect those conventions: breaking them without good reason simply opens us up to criticism and distracts from the content of the report.

Where our findings are likely to be contentious, we may need to be diplomatic. This should not, however, compromise clarity: if the project has issues, they should be clearly labelled as such. As my friend Payson Hall says, 'Be diplomatic, but not subtle.'

Finally, we should avoid blaming. We want our reports to trigger action to address the project's issues, not witch hunts. The best way to do this is to focus on what is happening on the project, how it got to be this way, and what could be done to improve things. (Avoiding blaming does not mean that we should avoid setting our findings into context. People may need to understand how issues arose, both to accept our findings and to take appropriate action. For example, if the original assumptions proved unfounded, we should say so: this may influence areas of the project outside our review.)

ENGAGING IN DIALOGUE

A report is one point in an ongoing dialogue. As we write it, we should be checking our facts with the project manager and team, and beginning to alert our sponsor and other stakeholders to the main findings. Such a dialogue serves two purposes: it gives us an opportunity to refine and correct our findings and gather supporting evidence, and it helps our audience to understand and accept the report. Ideally, there will be no major surprises by the time we come to submit the final report: people will be aware of at least the broad thrust of our findings. Again, this is especially important if they are likely to be contentious.

It can also be worthwhile backing our report with presentations, informal briefings, mentoring, and so on. As well as giving people an opportunity to ask questions, such sessions help us to check that our message has been heard correctly.

The case study *Earthquakes in the Project Portfolio* illustrates the effectiveness of taking this dialogue to the extreme. By publishing our findings openly and updating them each week to reflect new inputs, we created an incentive for people to discuss them and provide us with additional information. This proved to be a very effective way to create visibility in the organization's projects. The best mechanism for such dialogue will differ in every organization: it's worth identifying the feedback loops that operate within your organization and tapping into them.

One final point to remember: this dialogue helps the immediate audience to understand our report, but it's the report itself that will be archived. It still needs to be clear enough that future readers, for example at subsequent reviews, will understand it.

BUILDING CREDIBILITY

The credibility of the review team has a strong influence on whether their findings are accepted. There is no shortcut to building such credibility: it will come from a track record of effective reviews that produce useful outputs. However, there are some things we can do to accelerate the process:

- Build trust through openness. Be clear about our objectives and processes. If reviewers gain a reputation for having hidden agendas, people will always treat their findings with suspicion.

- Listen. People will place far more credence in a review team if they recognize that it has listened carefully and considered everything it has heard as it framed its findings.

- Let people find their own solutions. Reviewers add most value by listening to people and helping them to see what is really going on. Our interpretations and recommendations may add further value, but only if they don't get in the way of the solutions that people generate for themselves.

- Focus on learning and feedback. Prompt, direct feedback is easier to act on, so where possible we should provide findings as quickly as possible, and directly to the people who can act on them. And remember that feedback goes both ways – it's worth asking how we could improve our effectiveness as reviewers.

TRACKING ACTION

Finally, it is worthwhile to track the actions that result from our reviews. Do people act on our findings? Do these actions benefit the project? By building a mechanism to track the outcomes of our recommendations, we can:

- Ensure that busy project sponsors, managers and teams don't ignore or overlook important actions.

- Maximize the value from our investment in reviews. If people don't act on the findings, then why bother to make this investment in the first place?

- Refine the review process. Monitoring outcomes helps to identify where reviews are adding most value, and where the process can be improved.

- Demonstrate the value being delivered by reviews. Again, this helps us prioritize our investment in reviews against investment in other activities.

Actions will generally be recorded into the project's action register or some similar mechanism, with the project manager being responsible for overseeing their implementation. Where the project is being reviewed regularly, reviewers can confirm that these actions have been performed at the next review point. For one-off reviews, it may be useful to schedule a follow-up session to confirm that the actions have been performed. If possible, as well as confirming that the action has been performed, we should try to assess what benefit it provided to the project.

It may also be worthwhile to maintain a central record of actions and their impacts. This then provides information to monitor the effectiveness of the review process, and to manage checklists and other assets as discussed in Chapter 5. (We need to be pragmatic here: building a substantial database to track actions is only likely to be worthwhile in an organization that is investing significant effort in reviewing a large portfolio of projects. For many organizations, a simple spreadsheet will suffice.)

Software Review and Inspection Techniques

The software engineering literature has identified a number of techniques for quality review of artefacts produced during the software development lifecycle – specifications, designs, code and suchlike. Most of these techniques are directly applicable when reviewing other project documents (business cases, project plans, and so on). Their underlying principles also apply to most aspects of project reviews.

Weigers (2002) identifies five broad types of review, based on the purpose for which they are undertaken:

- Educational: The review is conducted to bring people up to speed with some aspect of the project. For example, a development team might walk through the system specification prior to commencing design, to ensure they have a common understanding.

- Peer: The author's peers help assess the quality of the artefact, and identify ways in which it could be improved.

- Post project: The review is conducted after the project in order to capture lessons for the future.

- Status: The review assesses the current status and risks for a project.

- Gate: The review provides information to senior managers to help them decide whether the project should proceed to the next phase.

Peer review underpins most scientific and academic progress. In the software engineering context, Weigers identifies seven approaches to peer review, based on the degree of formality applied to the review process:

- Inspection: A highly formal review with well-defined roles and procedures covering preparation for and conduct of the review. Inspection techniques (e.g. Fagan, 1976; Gilb and Graham, 1993) typically define rigorous entry and exit criteria for each review, together with protocols for managing checklists, capturing data, reporting, calculating metrics, and so on. Inspections can be very effective at finding defects and eliminating the root causes of these defects, but they require substantial organizational commitment and investment.

- Team review: A structured walkthrough with many aspects of an inspection, but with less rigorous separation of roles. The PRINCE2 Quality Review Technique equates approximately to such a review.

- Walkthrough: An informal review where the author describes their product to a group of peers and gathers their feedback. Roles, procedures, exit criteria, checklists and suchlike are less formally defined than for an inspection or team review. Walkthroughs can cover work products more rapidly than formal inspections, but are less likely to identify defects. Many project reviews operate at about this level of rigour, with project managers describing the project to a group of peers and hence obtaining their feedback.

- Pair programming: This is a technique, derived from Extreme Programming (Beck and Andres, 2004), whereby two people work together to develop an artefact, typically code. Only one person would be coding at any point, with the other observing, questioning assumptions and otherwise providing support. This means that there is a continuous, informal review of the artefact as it is developed.

- Peer deskcheck: The author simply asks another person to review their artefact. This can be done quickly and cheaply. It can be a good way to find obvious defects, but the lack of formality reduces the depth of the review and hence the overall number of defects likely to be found.

- Passaround: The author forwards their work product to several other people, asking for feedback. This is similar to a peer deskcheck, but with several reviewers.

- Ad hoc review: The author makes an ad hoc request to a peer, asking for help to find a particular defect or otherwise resolve an issue.

It can be seen that this spectrum balances a trade-off between rigour and coverage for any given review. Formal reviews entail greater investment in preparation and review time, and in supporting training, metrics, and so on. However, they repay this investment through their greater effectiveness at uncovering defects. Less formal reviews are easier to set up and can cover ground quickly, but are only likely to identify the more obvious issues. Thus, many organizations use a mixture of approaches: formal inspections for critical or high-risk work products, with walkthroughs or deskchecks for more routine artefacts. Alternatively, Gilb and Graham (1993) suggest an approach based on statistical sampling: the rigorous data capture associated with inspections means that it can be effective to inspect a sample of a project's work products, and then to base quality assurance decisions on this sample.

Beyond this trade-off between rigour and coverage, team and organizational culture will influence the approach used for reviewing. Some organizations naturally lean towards formal processes and capture of extensive data and metrics, while others favour ad hoc collaboration. Open source software development, for example, often favours informal reviews (the distributed nature of the teams makes formal review difficult), with the large number of potential reviewers compensating for the lack of formal process.

Gaps and Overlaps in Governance

Projects often seem to expose gaps in organizational governance. Being temporary endeavours, they may not align well to authority structures defined along traditional functional, geographical or other lines. This can leave project and other managers unclear about who is responsible for managing priorities and resources.

Organizations may adopt matrix or projectized structures to resolve some of these issues. Likewise, they may set up a Project Management Office (or some other variant of the PMO) to manage some of the conflicts and overlaps. However, this may not be appropriate for many organizations, and even where it is, there may be residual fuzziness in the decision-making structures.

As reviewers, we need to be able to deal with the issues this fuzziness can create, for two reasons. First, the consequences of unclear decision-making structures – resource conflicts, unclear priorities, and so on – can have a large impact on projects. We need to be able to recognize situations where our projects are exposed to this risk. Second, we need to be able to escalate such issues to the appropriate authorities when they do occur.

Organizational governance is a large subject. A host of laws and regulations (Sarbanes-Oxley, The Companies Act, Data Protection Act, Basel II, and so on) deal with elements of it. Likewise a number of 'best practices' (e.g. ITIL (OCG, n.d.) PRINCE2, COBIT (ISACA, 2008) address aspects of it. I don't profess to be able to cover all this ground here. In this chapter, I will simply explore some ways in which the governance matrix introduced in Chapter 8 can be used to reflect on the issues that may arise when undertaking project reviews.

It's easy to get pulled into the weeds when discussing governance. Many of the regulations and 'best practices' go into great detail to define dozens (or even hundreds) of principles, processes and control objectives. Because each 'best practice' focuses on a different aspect of governance, these processes and principles often overlap and conflict. One benefit of the governance matrix, at least for me, is that it's simple. It gives me a tool to think about the intent of governance rather than the details. I can then start to apply this intent to my primary objective: helping projects to succeed.

PROJECT AND ORGANIZATIONAL GOVERNANCE

The three types of decision discussed in Chapter 8 – setting direction ('what'), implementation ('how') and assurance ('how do we know we're on course') – apply as much to organizational governance as they do to project governance. It's simply that the strategic scope of the decisions tends to be broader. Thus, at the organizational steering level we would expect to find bodies that align to each of these decision types. In most corporations, these are the corporate board (setting direction), the Chief Executive Officer (CEO) and executive directors (implementing) and the audit committee and associated auditors (assuring). Public and not-for-profit organizations generally have similar structures.

(At a higher level again, I believe the three decision types also apply to national governance. For example, the three branches of government defined in the US constitution – legislature, executive and judiciary – map at least approximately onto these decision types.)

Figure 9.1 illustrates how project governance fits into this broader framework. It can help to think of the governance matrix as a fractal, with different versions of it covering progressively narrower strategic scope. Thus, project governance provides a more detailed view of one subset of the overall organizational governance structure. It may also help to consider several levels of such drill-down – organizational governance providing the broad framework for programme and then ultimately project governance, for example. At each level, we have the same types of decisions to make, but with progressively narrower strategic scope.

Decisions then cascade down the hierarchy. Management-level decisions for a programme become steering-level decisions for the projects within the programme, and so on. In terms of the people and organizational units involved, the programme manager may well act as sponsor for some projects within the programme. As reviewers, we will then be assessing whether these linkages exist and are functioning effectively when we consider project governance and decision making. Likewise, we may need to determine which level of strategic scope applies to any issues that we identify, and escalate them accordingly.

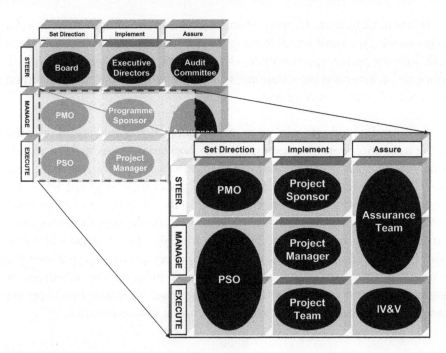

Figure 9.1   Fractal nature of governance

ASSURANCE WITH MULTIPLE SPONSORS

Under PRINCE2, project assurance is the responsibility of the project board. Thus, it is responsible for confirming that the view of project status it receives from the project manager is accurate, and that it understands the information it is receiving. Where the board lacks the time or expertise to do this, it may delegate assurance activities to an independent person or team. In this case, the sponsor of the project reviews should be clear: it's the project board.

This can become complex when the project board includes people from different organizations, with each member designating their own representative on the assurance team. In this case, different members of the assurance team may have different objectives: members representing the user perspective may be focused on product quality, for example, while those representing suppliers may be more interested in questions of compliance with contractual requirements. The assurance team may then try to cover too much ground in its reviews, thus failing to cover any area in adequate depth. At worst, a fragmented assurance team will disrupt the project team excessively and deliver conflicting messages to the different stakeholders. This negates the fundamental value of assurance, to deliver clean information.

This is most likely to happen when the board itself is fragmented. In such circumstances, the most effective thing an assurance team can probably do is work with the project sponsor to develop common purpose within the board. Failing this, it may need to escalate the issue to external executives: a fragmented board is itself a risk to any project.

A similar situation may arise when other organizational units are represented on the assurance team. For example, some assurance teams include people from areas such as audit and compliance, information security, and health and safety. In such cases, it is important to be clear about their reporting lines – do they report primarily to the project board, or to their functional management? Under what circumstances may they need to escalate through their functional management? It's certainly not impossible to make this arrangement work. Indeed, the additional functional expertise and perspective can enhance the assurance team's capabilities significantly, and merging the schedules of assurance, audit and other related activities can lessen the disruption to project teams. However, clarity of objectives and reporting lines is essential.

ASSURANCE AND THE PMO

The PMO typically provides a central pool of people with the necessary project management skills to undertake assurance and a good understanding of the organization's projects, methodology and standards. Thus, many organizations attempt to deliver assurance activities through the PMO. However, Figure 8.3 (page 190) suggests that the PMO occupies a different column in the governance matrix. What do we need to consider when setting up an assurance function within the PMO?

For a start, we need to be clear about which level of strategic scope the PMO is operating at, as discussed in Chapter 8. If the PMO is at the top left, setting priorities and allocating resources across the portfolio, then an assurance team within the PMO may be well placed to monitor ongoing alignment between projects and organizational objectives. Conversely, if the PMO as acting primarily as a support office, in the bottom left cell of the matrix, then a co-located assurance team is likely to focus on administrative efficiency within the projects it reviews. Is this the role we want our assurance team to fulfil?

Second, we need to protect the independence of the assurance team. As well as being independent of the projects it is reviewing, the assurance team needs to be independent of any supporting activities. For example:

- If the PMO is providing direct support to projects, for example, by operating processes such as status tracking, document management or configuration management, it can be difficult for a co-located assurance team to independently assess the effectiveness of these activities.

- If the PMO is setting standards and defining project management processes, there is a risk that a co-located assurance team will slip into an audit role, focusing too much on whether projects are following the PMO-defined processes. (At the same time, the assurance team will be well placed to understand the processes and the intent behind them, so may be a very effective mechanism for disseminating them as it conducts reviews and mentors project managers. This may well be an acceptable trade-off.)

As a rule of thumb, my experience is that an assurance team that is co-located with the PMO will have difficulty assessing activities at the same level of strategic scope as the PMO. However, it can usually assure activities at a lower level in the governance matrix. Thus, for example, an assurance team co-located with a portfolio management office (top left cell) will be able to assess individual projects within the portfolio, but it may not be sufficiently independent to adequately assess the effectiveness of the portfolio prioritization processes operated by the PMO itself. To assure these strategic-level processes, we need a truly independent unit.

To the extent that the PMO provides a 'spiritual home' for project managers – providing intellectual support and mentoring, defining career progression, and so on – it can also provide a home for project reviewers. If the PMO is also managing the organization's project management resource pool, then it may be well placed to manage the rotation of project managers through assurance teams. (As discussed in Chapters 10 and 11, such rotation can be a good way both to staff assurance teams and to extend project managers' experience and skills.) Thus, it may well be a pragmatic decision to co-locate the assurance function with the PMO. However, there may be some assurance activities that such a team will lack the independence to discharge effectively. For these activities, it may be necessary to gain assurance from another source, such as external consultants.

In general, assurance and the PMO complement each other. The PMO can be a valuable source of reference models for project reviewers, while the assurance team can help disseminate and assess the effectiveness of processes and standards defined by the PMO. They have a common interest in identifying and capturing good practice, and in ensuring the flow of clean information about projects. There are times, however, when they may need a clear separation of duties between setting standards and assuring that people are operating in alignment with these standards.

ASSURANCE AND OTHER STAFF OFFICES

Assurance teams may need to relate to staff offices beyond the PMO. Enterprise architecture teams, technical design authorities, process management centres of excellence, and suchlike, may all be responsible for setting direction and standards for some aspect of the organization's operations. These influence assurance in two ways:

- Reference models: The standards defined by such groups may be provide reference models for project reviews. Assurance teams therefore need to understand what standards are available and how they can be applied.

- Competing standards: It is easy for such offices to create competing and conflicting policies and standards. Assurance teams may need to deal with the issues this creates for projects (e.g. confusion about which standard applies, or cynicism about the value of central support and infrastructure).

Assurance teams are also well placed to identify examples of the impact of such standards on projects (either for benefit or for harm) and hence to provide an independent assessment of their utility. As described in Chapter 5, assurance teams may also support dissemination of practices defined by such groups. Thus there are many good reasons for assurance teams to develop good working relationships with such groups.

AUTHORITY OF THE ASSURANCE TEAM

Assurance teams sometimes seek authority to act directly on their findings, for example to halt or even cancel projects that they consider to be in trouble. The case study *Completion Bonds in the Film Industry* illustrates a situation where people in an assurance role have this authority. This certainly ensures that prompt action will be taken to implement the team's findings. However, it also risks placing the assurance team in a combative relationship with the project team, making it harder to obtain a realistic view of project status as people attempt to hide issues. (The review team may then attempt to use its authority to gain access to information. This creates further combativeness and hence escalates the situation. I've never found this to be a helpful dynamic.)

It may occasionally be appropriate for an assurance team populated by experienced, senior people to intervene directly when it identifies serious problems with a project. I personally favour maintaining a clear separation of duties between information gathering and direction setting. This forces the assurance team to focus on gathering sufficient evidence to make a case for action. Once the evidence is there, people will usually act.

DEALING WITH UNCLEAR OR FRAGMENTED GOVERNANCE

Even where lines of authority are well defined, it can be difficult to gather sufficient evidence and persuade sponsors to act. Where authority is unclear or people are not fulfilling their responsibilities, it can be even harder to prompt effective action. This may happen where roles and responsibilities are poorly defined, where gaps or conflicts exist in governance structures, or where there is frequent rotation of people through key roles. It is often a problem in consortia and joint ventures, especially in the early stages of their operation.

External review teams may not have sufficient context to recognize such issues in a short review. For example, the review sponsor may be unaware of the issues, or may have reasons to conceal them. However, consistent failure to act effectively on well-founded review findings will become clearer in the longer term. Such failure is likely to result from failures in the broader governance and management structures. In-house review teams are more likely to recognize these issues from the outset (provided they have not become inured to them through long exposure), but may not be well positioned to act on them.

Either way, there is no easy way that I know of for a review team to deal with such issues. Persuading people to allocate decision-making rights clearly, and to hold people to account for those decisions, can require patience, careful navigation of organizational power structures and perspectives, and the ability to tolerate fuzziness, ambiguity and frustration. At the same time, addressing these issues can add tremendous value: if governance is weak, most projects are going to struggle to succeed. Simply by recognizing the problem and drawing attention to it, assurance teams can do much to aid their projects.

Review Techniques in the Education Sector

Reviews and inspections are well established in the education sector. There is a substantial literature on peer reviews (e.g. Chism, 2007), and a number of well-documented frameworks for inspections (e.g. OFSTED , 2005 and OFSTED, 2006). These cover three broad types of review:

1.   peer review of teachers;

2.   peer review of publications;

3.   inspection of schools and other educational institutions.

These aren't project reviews, but there is much we can learn from the principles and practices established in the education sector. This case study summarizes some of those principles and practices.

WHY CONDUCT REVIEWS?

Reviews can be conducted for two reasons:

1.   Formative reviews help a person or organization identify ways to improve their performance. The review focuses on gathering examples that will give the reviewee insight into current issues and opportunities for improvement. The results would typically be kept confidential between the reviewer and the reviewee.

2.   Summative reviews grade the reviewee's performance against objective standards. They are performed to assure external stakeholders of the effectiveness of the person or institution being reviewed. The review focuses on gathering evidence to make the comparison, and would typically put its findings into the public domain.

There is general agreement that these two types of review, although they may use similar techniques, should be kept separate. In particular, many people are reluctant to share the detailed information required for formative reviews if they know this information will be also used for summative evaluation.

Reviews also deliver a number of other benefits. For example, reviewers learn about teaching techniques and practices by observing them in action, and by engaging in dialogue and reflection about their effectiveness. Likewise, establishing standards for reviews encourages people to think about and adopt good practices.

WHAT MAKES A REVIEW EFFECTIVE?

Four factors are necessary for an effective review:

1. A systematic process for identifying, gathering and assessing evidence: The type of evidence being gathered maps onto the objectives for the review. There is a well-defined plan for gathering this evidence, and clear standards for assessing it. This plan is backed by appropriate tools (e.g. checklists) and adequate time and resources.

2. Reviewers seen to have appropriate expertise, both in conducting reviews and in the domain being reviewed: Where necessary, there are multiple reviewers, both to bring the appropriate expertise and to reduce the impact of personal biases.

3. Institutional support for the review process: There are clear objectives for the overall process, with appropriate sponsorship. There is provision to learn from experience in order to improve the review process itself.

4. Active management of buy-in from all key stakeholders: Objectives and standards for reviews are seen to be fair and are openly communicated to all concerned. Confidentiality, of reviewee and reviewer, is managed appropriately.

AN EXAMPLE OF THE INSPECTION PROCESS

OFSTED has been inspecting schools in England since the early 1990s. Inspections complement a school's self-evaluation and improvement processes by providing an independent evaluation of its strengths and weaknesses in five areas:

1.   quality of education provided;

2.   level of achievement by the school's pupils;

3.   quality of management and leadership;

4.   capacity to accurately self-assess performance and hence make improvements;

5.   efficiency of resource management.

Inspections are short, focused exercises, typically lasting two days and happening every three years (more frequently for schools that are causing concern, less frequently in strong schools). They are scheduled with very short notice. This is intended to reduce disruption to the school: schools are not expected to do a lot of preparation for an inspection.

The inspection team contact the school about two to five days before the inspection in order to agree schedules and arrangements. The inspectors then use the school's management plan, self-evaluation forms, the results of previous inspections, and the results of surveys of parents' and pupils' views to frame hypotheses to be pursued during the inspection. The lead inspector delivers this assessment to the school's leadership team on the afternoon before the inspection and works with them to identify the best way to gather evidence to explore the hypotheses.

During the inspection itself, the inspectors aim to gather sufficient evidence to make a fair assessment of the school's overall effectiveness, and of its strengths and weaknesses. This evidence is gathered by observing classes, talking to staff and pupils, analysing pupils' work and records, tracking key processes, and meeting with the school's management. It is recorded against a standard framework of questions on pre-defined evidence forms.

As the inspection progresses, the inspection team use the emerging findings to steer their investigations. They also discuss their findings with the headteacher, senior managers and governors, giving them an opportunity to respond and to identify additional sources of evidence. The inspectors may also give oral feedback to teachers and staff where appropriate.

At the end of the inspection, the team agree an overall judgement of the school's effectiveness, graded against a common scale used for all inspections. This is provided as oral feedback at the end of the on-site inspection, followed by a written report issued within three weeks. This report is in standard format, no longer than 2,000 words, and must be 'well argued, written in plain English and based convincingly on the evidence'. The school's parents are the main audience for the report. (A pre-publication draft of the report is also sent to the school, to ensure factual accuracy. If the school disagrees with the inspectors' judgements, it must provide evidence to back its case.)

This inspection process is relatively formal, because of the need to provide consistency across a large number of schools and inspection teams (and because school inspection operates in a highly politicized environment). Consistency is also assured by a variety of quality assurance processes: independent assessments of the effectiveness of inspectors, inspections and reports; post-inspection surveys; a well-defined process for handling complaints about inspections. Inspectors are also expected to undergo extensive training (several months, including placements) before conducting inspections, and then to engage in ongoing continuing professional development.

Most project reviews will not need this level of formality (although some might, for example where a project is subject to legal dispute or intense politicking). Nonetheless, this example illustrates a number of practices that any review team might consider:

- The provision of extensive training for reviewers, coupled with well-defined feedback processes to improve the conduct of reviews.

- An emphasis on systematic gathering and assessment of evidence.

- The use of explicit hypotheses to focus the review team's attention.

- Independent assessments as part of an overall process of monitoring and improvement. Inspections complement the school's own self-assessment processes, for example, and where these processes are proving to be effective, the need for independent assessments is lessened accordingly.

PART IV

Running an Assurance Team

The final set of challenges that review and assurance teams face is organizational. Reviewers can feel isolated and outside mainstream career paths, with little support as they attempt to raise complex (and often contentious) issues with the projects they're reviewing. Likewise, organizations often struggle with questions such as how much to invest in assurance activities, how to manage this budget, and what support structures to put in place.

This section looks at some of the factors that need to be considered when setting up a project review or assurance function within an organization.

Chapter 10 looks at these factors from the organizational perspective. It outlines an approach to setting up a project review process within an organization, then discusses some of the debates and trade-offs you may need to address as you do this. It considers issues such as establishing the business case for reviews, what type of reviews to perform and how to manage concerns such as confidentiality and independence.

Chapter 11 looks at these concerns from the perspective of the individual reviewer or review team. It considers the type of stresses that a review team may experience and how to build support structures to manage these stresses. It also thinks a little about the types of skills that reviewers may need, and about how these skills might be built.

Chapter 12 then recaps the key messages of this book.

Organizational Issues

CHAPTER

10

Setting up a project review process can entail substantial commitment from the organization. Senior people need to be freed from project activities in order to undertake reviews. Investment may need to be made in training and support structures. How do we balance this investment against other options, such as project management training? Project managers may feel that the process signals lack of trust in their capabilities and their willingness to share accurate status information. How do we deal with these concerns?

This chapter looks at some of the issues that assurance team managers and sponsors may need to manage as they build the review process and interact with other parts of the organization. It looks first at some of the key steps that might be undertaken when setting up a review process: establishing a business case, selecting projects for review, defining the review process and parameters. It then looks at some of the trade-offs that will need to be managed as the process is defined, and at some of the critical success factors and risks for establishing the process.

Much of this material builds from the discussions in earlier chapters. This chapter brings those discussions together from the perspective of the organization that is establishing a new (or renewed) review process.

ESTABLISHING A REVIEW PROCESS

Many organizations start to think about project reviews, then do very little. Perhaps they write review points into their standard project lifecycle then leave it for project managers to organize the reviews for themselves. Perhaps they designate someone to coordinate reviews in amongst all their other duties. In the end, project managers who are committed to reviews ensure that their projects are reviewed. Most other projects proceed with little external scrutiny or feedback. (And it's probably these latter projects that most need feedback.) These organizations find it easier to blame project managers for failure than to invest systematically in reviews.

To break out of this dynamic, I find it useful to go through the stages identified in Table 10.1. If this looks like the outline for a project plan, that's because it is. The balance of this chapter discusses some of the key trade-offs and success factors involved in executing such a project.

THE BUSINESS CASE FOR REVIEWS

Most organizations will require a clear business case before investing in a sustained programme of reviews. Even if no-one is demanding a documented business case, it is worth preparing one for two reasons:

1. A well-defined business case can help sustain the programme when it runs into difficulties. Without such clarity, review teams can find themselves fighting constant battles simply to justify their own existence.

2. The business case will give us parameters to steer the programme by. As we make decisions about which projects to review, what type of reviews to conduct and how to allocate resources to the different reviews, the reasoning behind the business case will suggest options and priorities.

To prepare this case, we need to make two key decisions – what do we want to achieve from the programme, and how much should we invest in it? These then drive the overall ROI.

OBJECTIVES AND BENEFITS

A review and assurance programme can deliver benefits in three broad areas: avoiding issues within individual projects; better decision making across the project portfolio; and better dissemination of skills and good practices across the organization. Looking at each of these in turn:

1. By identifying potential issues on projects and addressing them before they blow up, we can look for benefits such as:

    •   Reduced delay and budget overrun: Many issues can be fixed much more quickly and cheaply if they are addressed early. Conversely, last minute fixes often entail higher coordination overheads, overtime, penalty charges from suppliers, and so on.

Table 10.1 Establishing a review process

Stage	Key issues

1. Build the business case

- How do we set and agree clear objectives for the review process?
- How much should we invest in reviews?
- How do we establish potential return on investment (ROI)?

2. Establish ownership of the review process

- Who is the executive sponsor for the process?
- What does the sponsor need to do to encourage adoption of the process?
- What does the sponsor need to do to ensure that benefits are realized (e.g. that project teams act on the findings of reviews)?
- Who will manage day-to-day operation of the process?

3. Establish strategy for rolling out the process

- Where do we start? For example, which projects will we focus on?
- How will we extend the process to other projects?

4. Establish operational parameters for reviews

- Which projects should be reviewed?
- What sort of reviews should be undertaken for these projects?
- How frequently should we conduct reviews?
- What evidence do we need to gather, and how will we gather it?
- How will we manage concerns such as confidentiality?

5. Establish review teams and processes

- What mixture of peer reviewers and dedicated assurance teams should we use?
- How will we manage people's time, especially for part-time reviewers, technical specialists and senior stakeholders?
- What training do reviewers need?
- How will we manage career planning, incentives, and so on, for reviewers?
- How will we establish a good working relationship between review teams and the projects they're reviewing?
- How will we create and manage review assets and tools (checklists, for example)?
- How will we coordinate reviews?

6. Propagate and sustain the process

- How will we monitor the effectiveness of reviews, and the benefits they're delivering?
- How will we communicate success stories more widely?
- How will we learn from experience and improve the process?

- Reduced spend on abandoned projects: How much would the organization save if it could identify and cancel failing projects sooner?

- Enhanced reputation with key stakeholders: For example, customers will appreciate more consistent delivery of project outputs; analysts will appreciate greater predictability of cashflow. This could lead to enhanced sales or reduced costs for relationship and reputation management.

- Reduced costs due to reduced staff burnout and turnover: Late and troubled projects can have a serious impact on their teams: long hours, stress, low morale. Reducing the incidence of such projects can reduce many of the indirect costs associated with these issues.

2. By providing better information to people making decisions at the portfolio level, we can look for benefits such as:

- Better resource allocation across the portfolio: For example, by reducing our commitment to failing projects we can free up resources for other projects, thus delivering their benefits more quickly.

- Improved management of the impacts of delayed projects: For example, projects that are dependent on the outputs of a delayed project can implement contingency plans earlier and in a more controlled way, thus reducing their costs.

- Greater confidence to initiate high-risk/high-reward projects.

- Reduced uncertainty and infighting amongst decision makers: This can itself reduce the amount of effort needed to manage the portfolio, and free up decision makers to focus on other areas.

3. By improving the dissemination of skills and good practices, we can aim to improve the effectiveness of our project teams and the overall efficiency of project delivery.

An effective review programme is likely to focus on one area at a time. If we try to achieve too much at once, we risk diffusing our effort. We also risk creating conflicting reporting lines for the review teams. Focusing on project-level benefits means that their primary audience should be project managers or sponsors. Focusing on portfolio-level benefits suggests they should report primarily to senior executives. Trying to do both at once is a recipe for confusion.

Once we've decided where to focus, we can set clear, measurable objectives. We can also identify which stakeholders will benefit most from the initiative: these are the people we can start to enlist to support the programme.

HOW MUCH? WHO PAYS?

How much should we invest in reviews? There are no well-defined benchmarks that I know of, and the amount to invest will clearly depend on the context: an organization with a large number of mission-critical projects has much more interest in assuring their delivery than an organization running a few, small projects.

The case study *Completion Bonds in the Film Industry* does give a useful benchmark. If financiers there are prepared to pay between 2 per cent and 6 per cent of the project budget for a completion guarantee, that puts an upper bound on what it's worth investing in reviews. More or less mature industries may have different figures, but 2 per cent of budget is probably a reasonable upper bound for most projects. My experience is certainly that 0.5 per cent to 2 per cent of budget is a reasonable level of investment for software development projects, depending on how complex and mission-critical they are.

I'd therefore base my initial case on a range of scenarios: 0.5 per cent of project budget might buy a moderate level of assurance for high-risk or high-impact projects; 2 per cent of budget might buy in-depth assurance for these projects and a lighter level for other projects in the portfolio; 1 per cent buys somewhere in between. If I have a well-quantified view of the likely benefits, I may be able to identify an appropriate level of investment from this planning. In practice, it's rare to have sufficiently reliable data to do this, so I'd probably start small: focus assurance activities on high-risk and high-impact projects, then extend the initiative as we prove benefits and build our skills pool.

This raises the question of how to fund the assurance activities. Table 10.2 maps out three common options and their strengths and weaknesses. The overall objectives for the initiative will influence the option chosen. Funding assurance as a central overhead is particularly appropriate when the assurance team reports to central executives: they are then paying for the information they want. Funding it out of project budgets may make more sense when assurance focuses on helping individual projects.

Table 10.2   Options for funding a review or assurance programme

Option	Benefits	Risks
1. Assurance is a central overhead, funded from a separate budget.	• Projects do not cut assurance activities when trying to reduce their budgets. • Assurance function has a clear view of its overall budget, to fund training and similar non-project activities. • Assurance is clearly independent of the project teams.	• Assurance teams do not need to demonstrate value to project teams: their accountability is solely to central budget holders. • Projects neglect to budget the time their own team needs to spend interacting with assurance teams (e.g. in interviews; in following up findings and actions). • Assurance budget is at risk of broader organizational budget cuts.
2. Assurance is funded by a mandatory 'tax' on project budgets.	• As for option 1, plus: • Assurance budget is more visible to project teams, hence they are more likely to plan their own time to work with review teams and gain value from assurance.	• Project budget holders resist the mandatory 'tax'.
3. Assurance is an optional service. Projects that want it purchase it from their own budgets.	• Assurance teams must actively demonstrate the value they are delivering to projects. This can help build working relationships between assurance and project teams, making it easier to conduct effective reviews. • Projects that do purchase assurance are likely to be committed to following up on its findings.	• Many projects (including those which most need it) may not purchase assurance. • The need to satisfy project 'customers' may jeopardize the independence of assurance teams' findings. • There is no clear, long-term view of the assurance budget, so it is hard to maintain the skills pool and invest in activities such as training.

RETURN ON INVESTMENT

Once we have identified the benefits we will focus on and the level of investment we wish to make, calculating ROI should be relatively straightforward. However, a number of factors can complicate the calculations:

- Availability of baseline data: Many organizations lack clear data on the direct and indirect costs of project overruns and delays.

- Ability to quantify likely benefits: Some of the potential benefits (e.g. enhanced reputation or improved decision making) are difficult to quantify. Even if a way to quantify them can be agreed, there is often no easy way to identify the likely degree of improvement that reviews will make.

- Gathering evidence to substantiate the figures: Sources such as case studies and surveys may give some data to estimate the potential benefits, but these don't always translate well between organizations. Some benefits are very sensitive to organizational context.

In the absence of good data, we may need to make informed estimates for these figures. Nonetheless, it's still worth thinking about how to quantify benefits. This both forces us to think through what we're trying to achieve, and helps us to set up a strategy for monitoring benefits delivery. This monitoring strategy will in turn help us to steer the initiative: we can compare benefits delivered against the original estimates and hence identify whether our original assumptions or approach need to be changed. (This implies, of course, that our assurance teams will invest some effort in tracking the benefits they're delivering.)

Developing ROI calculations is often iterative: we refine our objectives and budget in response to the initial calculations, and hence optimize the potential ROI.

PLACEBO EFFECT

One final point about benefits: some of the benefits may well come from a type of placebo effect. When projects are subject to regular independent reviews, people may set up their projects with a little more care in the first place. They may also take time to reflect and self-evaluate prior to reviews, hence identifying and fixing issues before the reviews take place. These benefits result from the review programme, but it is very difficult for reviewers to identify and track them.

OWNERSHIP OF THE REVIEW PROCESS

Strong sponsorship can make life much easier for review teams. The sponsor is likely to be active in two areas:

26   PROJECT REVIEWS, ASSURANCE AND GOVERNANCE

1.   Selling the review process to project sponsors and other executives.

2.   Ensuring that projects act on the findings from reviews. Although review teams should be able to negotiate this directly with project managers in most cases, having an effective escalation path can be useful. (However, as discussed in earlier chapters, if this escalation needs to be used frequently, there may be wider problems.)

This suggests that the ideal sponsor will operate at a similar (or higher) level to most project sponsors within the organization. This both gives them access to project sponsors and other executives, and signals that the organization is taking reviews seriously. They should also be someone who project sponsors and managers will listen to, and should be able to convey enthusiasm for the review process. Finally, they will probably need considerable political and interpersonal skills to deal with the projects that get escalated to them.

ROLL-OUT STRATEGY

The shape of the organization's project portfolio and the objectives for the review programme will determine where we start with reviews and how we roll them out from there. There are two broad options: start with a small set of projects and then extend the programme to address progressively more projects, or start with a single type of review and then extend the programme to include additional types. If our emphasis is capturing and disseminating good practice, for example, we may begin by reviewing the most innovative projects. If our emphasis is addressing a small set of problems that is common to most projects in the organization, we might start by setting up a well-defined gateway that applies to all projects and then gradually extend our reviews across the project lifecycle.

In general, however, I favour starting with a small team of senior reviewers and focusing attention on high-value or high-risk projects. This is where we're most likely to be able to demonstrate value and hence build momentum for a wider roll-out. By starting with a small team, we can also defer investment in tools such as issue-tracking databases: a small team can operate fairly informally as it establishes and refines its processes. We then capture these processes into more formal tools and training once they've been proven. Finally, a small, senior team is generally best placed to establish good working relationships with project teams, managers and sponsors. These initial relationships will then help us to expand the programme more widely.

REVIEW PARAMETERS

SELECTING PROJECTS FOR REVIEW

Chapter 2 discussed criteria for determining how much effort to invest in reviewing each project. Several of the case studies also address this question. *Formal Gateways in the Public Sector* illustrates the use of checklists to determine what level of independent assurance is needed for a project. *Review Techniques in the Education Sector* illustrates the use of outcomes from previous reviews and self-assessments to determine the frequency with which inspections should be conducted. As we set up our review programme, we will need to determine which criteria work best for our organization.

WHAT TYPE OF REVIEW TO PERFORM

If there's one message I'm trying to deliver through this book, it's that there is no single way to conduct a project review. Different approaches to reviewing achieve different objectives. Most organizations will need to develop a portfolio of different review types, as illustrated in the case study *Assuring Fixed Price Implementations*.

Chapters 2 through 4 discussed parameters that need to be considered as we do this – the timing of reviews, degree of formality and independence, focus areas, and so on. Two the most important trade-offs – degree of independence and timing of reviews – are discussed below.

INDEPENDENT ASSURANCE OR PEER REVIEW?

The answer to this question determines whether we need to staff a distinct assurance team, or will focus more on coordinating peer reviewers drawn from existing projects. Table 10.3 examines the trade-offs.

It can be seen that both approaches have benefits. The most important factor is probably whether we are focusing on formative or summative reviews. If a project begins to get off course, is it more important to get it back on course or to let other people know so they can adjust their plans? If the former, review teams can focus on formative reviews. If the latter, they will need to focus more on summative reviews, and a higher degree of independence is likely to be required.

Of course, it's possible to mix the two modes. Peer review teams can be drawn from people in other business units, for example, to enhance their independence. Or review teams can contain a mixture of peers and independent specialists. Some reviews may be conducted by peers while others are conducted by an

Table 10.3   Independent assurance or peer review?

	Peer review	Independent assurance
Description	*Teams of reviewers are drawn from other projects in order to conduct reviews.*	*Dedicated reviewers spend a significant proportion of their time conducting review and assurance activities. (These reviewers may specialize in assurance, or they may rotate through the assurance team, perhaps on six or 12 month secondments.)*
Availability of reviewers	Reviewers must take time from their own projects to conduct reviews. This can make it difficult to get reviewers for some reviews.	Dedicated staff are more likely to be available for reviews, although this may need some coordination when reviewers cover multiple projects.
Skills of reviewers	Non-specialist reviewers may take an unstructured approach to reviews, with consequent risk of overlooking issues. (Training and mentoring can reduce this risk.)	Specialist reviewers are more likely to adopt a rigorous approach, and are able to develop skills in areas such as assessing projects quickly, gathering evidence, and conducting interviews.
Understanding of projects	Reviewers are able to connect to project teams, as they're managing similar projects themselves.	Reviewers risk losing touch with hands-on aspects of managing projects.
Understanding of potential issues		Reviewers see many projects, so quickly develop a sense of what type of issues to look for.
Relationship to project team	Reviewers can usually develop an open, friendly relationship with project teams as they share experiences. This can help them to gather information about the project, but also creates a risk that reviewers will be reluctant to challenge their peers too strongly.	Reviewers risk developing an adversarial relationship with project teams. (Staffing the team with respected people with good interpersonal skills helps manage this risk.)
Organizational learning	Can be a good way to share experiences across projects and thus promote organizational learning.	Reviewers risk becoming focused on assessing projects rather than disseminating learning.
Match to overall objectives	Peer review works well when the primary objective is to support organizational learning by sharing experiences across projects. It can also be a good way to conduct formative reviews (helping project teams and sponsors to improve their performance). Peer reviewers can also conduct summative reviews, but the above risks then need to be managed carefully.	Independent assurance works well when the primary objective is to provide independently validated information to executives and other stakeholders. Summative reviews (e.g. gateways to support strict go/no-go decisions) are well suited to independent assurance. Assurance teams can also conduct formative reviews, provided they are kept separate from the summative activities.

independent team. Case studies such as *Formal Gateways in the Public Sector* and *Assuring Fixed Price Implementations* illustrate all of these possibilities.

One final consideration: independent assurance teams tend to have higher (or at least more visible) support costs.

TIMING AND FREQUENCY OF REVIEWS

Chapter 2 identified three overall options for the timing of reviews – periodic, event based and ad hoc. Which of these options do we want to use, and when? This generally boils down to a decision between two approaches. Some organizations favour structured gate reviews at a small number of points in the project lifecycle. Others favour smaller, more frequent reviews throughout the project. Table 10.4 outlines some of the trade-offs here.

Fortunately, it's not an all-or-nothing decision: many organizations use a mixture of both approaches. e.g. see the case studies *Earthquakes in the Project Portfolio* and *Assuring Fixed Price Implementations*.)

Likewise, both approaches can be supplemented by ad hoc reviews and health checks when necessary. Such health checks tend to have similar attributes to gate reviews: they provide a deep snapshot of the project's status at a point in time. They do have the added complication that, being unscheduled, they can create concerns about the project: some people interpret the need for a health check as a sign that the project is in trouble. The review team may need to manage this perception when they brief the project team.

On balance, I tend to favour regular, small reviews. Their ability to spot trends as they develop means that issues can be addressed before they grow. Regular reviews also create a rapid feedback loop to the project team: this aids team learning considerably. Another benefit of regular reviews is that people get plenty of practice, and hence get better at reviewing. (This benefits both the review team and the project team.)

If we are conducting regular reviews, we next need to decide how frequently to conduct them. This is generally determined by the project. Rapidly moving, agile projects may benefit from a review every couple of weeks (often linked to the end of each iteration). For projects that are moving more slowly, four or six weeks may be the appropriate interval. The key question here is: how quickly do we need to be able to spot trends in the project? It generally takes at least a couple of reviews to spot an emerging trend, so reviewing every month means that we may not recognize some issues for two or three months. On a

Table 10.4   Gate or regular review?

	Gate review	Regular review
Description	Structured reviews are conducted at defined points in the project lifecycle, for example at transition points between phases.	Reviews are conducted at regular intervals throughout the project.
Depth of review	Reviews tend to be fairly substantial events, involving interviews, scrutiny of deliverables, and so on. Thus, they will examine the project in some depth.	Reviews tend to be more lightweight: often little more than a single meeting where people walk through a checklist. Thus, they risk missing less obvious issues.
Ability to track trends in the project	Reviews are infrequent, so will generally not spot trends until they are well developed. Instead, reviews give a deep snapshot of the project's state at a point in time.	Frequent reviews allow reviewers to spot trends (e.g. small slippages that may eventually accumulate into a major issue) as they develop.
Overhead for reviewers	Reviewers are not familiar with the project, so a significant part of their time may be spent getting up to speed with project objectives and approach.	Reviewers become familiar with the project over time, so can focus their attention on assessing the current state.
Overhead for project teams	Reviews are relatively disruptive to the project team (e.g. to assemble materials and attend interviews) when they happen, but happen infrequently. (The materials required for each review should be drawn from standard project artefacts: review teams should, in general, not ask projects to create special materials just for the review.) When gate reviews inform major decisions about the project, project teams sometimes spend a lot of time ensuring they get the 'right result' from the review.	Each review entails relatively little disruption to the project team, but there are more reviews.
Objectivity of reviewers	Reviewers are generally well separated from the project team, hence able to maintain an objective view of the project.	Reviewers meet regularly with the project team, so may risk 'going native' as they develop relationships and become accustomed to the project team's approach and prejudices.
Need for specialist skills on review team	In order to conduct an in-depth assessment, the review team may need to call on technical and other specialists at some points.	Because reviews focus on monitoring trends rather than in-depth assessment at any point, they may need fewer specialist technical skills.

12-month project, that may still give us time to get back on course. On a three-month project, the issue could well delay the project before our reviews spot it. For reviews to be fully effective in this latter case, they need to happen more frequently.

The optimum frequency for reviews will also be influenced by the effectiveness of the project's status reporting. If the project team demonstrates an accurate perception of its status, risks and issues through its regular reports and self-assessments, we may choose to reduce the frequency of external reviews, and to focus them on assessing the continued effectiveness of the project's internal monitoring. (The case study *Review Techniques in the Education Sector* illustrates this approach.)

Finally, regular reviews need to be linked into the project plans. (Gate reviews are automatically linked to the project plans: by definition, they happen at particular project milestones.) This may mean no more than scheduling a regular review meeting, or we may benefit from tighter integration. For example, it may help to adjust the review schedule so that project reviews follow internal quality reviews: we will then be assessing project status based on an informed view of the quality of its outputs. For large or high-risk projects, it may be worthwhile to develop an assurance plan specific to the project, both to ensure that external assurance activities happen at meaningful points and to allow the project team to plan their workload to accommodate reviews.

CONFIDENTIALITY

Should reviewers' discussions and reports be confidential, or should they be shared openly? This question has spawned numerous debates. *Formal Gateways in the Public Sector* illustrates a case where assuring the project team that information will be kept confidential makes it easier for people to discuss their concerns. In the case study *Earthquakes in the Project Portfolio*, on the other hand, open discussion of review findings created opportunities to gather fresh information and hence improve the findings. Factors to consider include:

- Ability to gather information: Some people will only open up when they are assured of confidentiality. In some organizations, this is a valid fear: bearers of bad news can be ostracized, or worse.

- Credence that can be placed in the information that is gathered: Some stakeholders may not accept or act on unattributed information – they may doubt its veracity, or be concerned about hidden agendas. Conversely, some people may struggle to get their views accepted:

       delivering their insight in unattributed form may be the only way to get it heard.

- Ability to act on findings: Publicizing an issue widely may make it difficult for the appropriate people to act. For example, senior stakeholders may interfere prematurely or political opponents may mobilize to exploit the problem.

- Legal issues: If the project is sensitive (e.g. highly confidential or under threat of litigation), your ability to share information may be constrained. Conversely, you can't promise confidentiality if you uncover illegal activity. In all such cases, the review team should seek legal advice as to how to record and disseminate its findings.

My experience is that openness begets openness. If reviewers put their information into the public domain, people will respond to correct errors, fill in gaps, identify related concerns and suggest alternative courses of action. This feedback improves the quality of the findings and recommendations. Unless there is a compelling reason to favour confidentiality, I therefore prefer openness.

(Many of the pressures favouring confidentiality stem from issues within the organizational culture – for example, lack of trust and inability to delegate effectively. When handling this debate, reviewers may need to decide whether they wish to effect cultural change, or whether simply helping projects to deliver more effectively within the current culture is a more realistic objective.)

ESTABLISHING TEAMS AND PROCESSES

Once we have defined the overall objectives and parameters for the review process, we can begin to staff our review teams and establish our working practices. This involves activity in three areas:

1. developing the community of reviewers;

2. developing relationships with other stakeholders;

3. developing review tools, working practices, and other assets.

Our community of reviewers includes the mix of peer reviewers and dedicated assurance staff, as discussed above. We must also build access to the technical and other specialists that we may call upon for some reviews. This pool of reviewers will need appropriate training (covering both the review process and softer skills such as interviewing and observation – see Chapter 11). For anyone who will spend a significant proportion of their time reviewing, we may need to adjust their job description and incentives to reflect their new responsibilities. We also need to consider reporting lines for reviewers, especially for dedicated assurance staff.

As we develop this community, we will also need to establish relationships with a variety of other stakeholders. Project sponsors and other executives need to understand how reviews affect them, and why. Project managers and teams need to start integrating reviews into their planning. At this point, we may run into one of the paradoxes of reviewing: reviews probably add most value for the weaker project managers and teams, yet it is these teams which are most likely to resist them. Strong teams are generally, although not always, happy to engage with external perspective and feedback on their work.

How do we deal with any resistance? It may be possible simply to use an executive mandate to force projects to accept reviews. This is particularly true when the overall objective is to improve information flow to senior executives, and in organizations with a very hierarchical culture. In most other circumstances, an executive mandate risks backfiring: projects may comply unenthusiastically, making it hard for reviewers to function effectively. It may therefore be better to back off and focus initially on the projects that will accept reviews. As we demonstrate value with those projects, we will earn the right to extend our activities to other projects. (This goes back to our roll-out strategy: starting with the enthusiasts and growing from there is often a viable strategy.)

Over time, we will develop a range of tools, checklists and standard working practices to support our reviews. As discussed in Chapter 5, we may begin with assets such as basic checklists, but they will become more valuable as we learn from experience and tailor them to our circumstances. So in this phase of the initiative, I'd focus my attention on building the review community and relationships, developing only a minimal subset of tools at this point.

PROPAGATE AND SUSTAIN THE PROCESS

The balance of the initiative is essentially about ongoing refinement and roll-out – conducting reviews, learning from the experience and hence improving the way we do reviews, and extending our coverage to additional projects and phases of the project lifecycle.

As we do this, it's worth gathering information about the conduct and effectiveness of reviews. For example, we may want to track:

- timing of reviews, matched to stage and type of project;

- resources invested in reviews (by reviewers, project teams and other stakeholders);

- outputs from reviews (issues identified, actions, project team satisfaction as measured by post-review feedback);

- results of the actions (Were they undertaken? What impact did this have on the project or organization? Can we quantify the benefits?);

- issues experienced by review teams.

The objective here is twofold. First, we want to gather evidence on the impact of reviews, both so we can demonstrate the value they are adding and in order to balance our investment between reviews and other project support activities. Second, we can use this information to improve the review process. (See also the discussion on managing checklists in Chapter 5.)

This information may eventually lead to a metrics database to help us quantify benefits and ROI. As noted above, however, I'd focus my energy initially on the softer side of reviews: building relationships and gathering success stories. Establishing a review process is far more about people and change management than it is about hard numbers.

GROWING ADOPTION

Each organization undergoes change in its own way. I can't give a general formula that will help you persuade people to perform and pay attention to project reviews. However, here are some factors that have worked for me:

- Listening: It's only when we demonstrably understand the issues that projects are dealing with that people will listen to us. If reviewers start by actively listening to people and trying to understand their concerns, they're much more likely to be able to persuade projects that they have something to offer.

- Starting where the organization is: Work out what the organization is good at, and what it isn't good at. (Tools such as maturity models might help here – see below.) Understand the culture. Likewise, understand your strengths and weaknesses as reviewers. Develop your approach to work from your own and the organization's strengths.

- Clear and clearly communicated objectives: If review teams gain a reputation for hidden agendas or biases, they will find it hard to engage effectively with project teams. Conversely, if they are seen as 'honest brokers', they are likely to be welcomed and consulted.

- Learning and adjusting the strategy: It's hard to get everything right first time. It's often more effective to try something, learn from the experience, and do it better the next time.

- Continuously demonstrating value: This both makes it easier to gather feedback and learn, and provides ammunition to deal with sceptics.

- Remembering that organizations change one person at a time. Every individual – executive, sponsor, manager or team member – will have different drivers and perspectives. We need to understand and engage with their individual drivers if we are to persuade them to change. This means listening to individuals and valuing their perspectives. Trying to change the whole organization at once, or even an entire project team, is generally too big a task for me to undertake successfully.

RISKS

What is going to derail the initiative? Again, every organization will be different, but here are some of the common risks I've come across:

- Cultural resistance: Reviews are about openness and sharing information. Some organizations have trouble with this. If this is the case, reviewers probably need to accept that they will make slow progress and pace themselves accordingly. Beyond that, it becomes even more important to demonstrate that you are prepared to listen to people and be an honest broker if you are to break through such cultural barriers.

- Lack of organizational commitment: This may show itself through symptoms such as failure to allocate sufficient resources to review teams, or lack of support from executives and sponsors to follow up on review findings. This may be a showstopper risk: if you have a clear business case and the organization still won't commit adequate resources, you may do more harm than good to continue with the initiative. Running a review programme without sufficient resources to do an adequate job risks creating a false sense of security: people may think their projects are being reviewed when they aren't.

- Resistance from project teams: Many people may resent the implication that they can't be trusted or need to be policed. As discussed above, the best strategy to deal with this is probably to back off and work initially with the people who are happy to engage. As you build a reputation for integrity and adding value, you will be able to extend your coverage.

- Project teams don't plan for reviews: Even where review teams do all they can to minimize disruption to projects, they will have some impact. People need to participate in interviews and suchlike. They need to act on the findings from reviews. If we're running peer review teams, people need to find time from their projects to participate in reviews of other projects. Review teams need to establish contact with project managers as early as possible, to help them plan for the impact of reviews.

- Using reviews to evaluate project managers or team members: If reviews are seen to be about evaluating people, these people will have an incentive to hide problems and focus on what's working well. This negates the value of project reviews.

- Becoming overly dependent on review teams: Projects can come to assume that assurance teams are doing all the necessary monitoring, and hence become more lax about status tracking and risk management. In extreme cases, project managers can become dependent on reviewers even to make decisions: major decisions are made at review meetings, with the project manager simply overseeing their execution. This robs the project of a day-to-day decision maker, and means that the reviewer can no longer be truly objective about the project. If review teams start to see this happening, they need to step back and clarify their role.

Finally, my colleague Bent Adsersen notes that people have often had the experience where feedback on a product or process has become conflated with feedback on the person who created the product. As a result, many people tend to avoid reviews, or else they avoid conveying difficult messages during reviews. Managers may then resist reviews, either because they are seen to add little value or because they risk opening complex interpersonal and intrateam disputes. This dynamic can be difficult to break. Again, my experience is that reviewers who are prepared to focus on listening to people and acting as honest brokers can eventually build sufficient trust to operate an effective review process. Conversely, reviewers who focus on trying to demonstrate how clever they are risk exacerbating the dynamic.

THE RISK OF SUCCESS

If reviews succeed, project teams may begin to rely on them to catch and address issues. For example:

- As discussed above, projects may get more lax with their planning, status tracking and risk management, expecting reviewers to catch any issues.

- Projects may become reliant on reviewers to communicate issues to executives and other stakeholders, rather than escalating them through their direct management chain.

Reviewers need to be clear that they are a complement to other project management practices, not a replacement for them. It can be tempting for reviewers to make themselves essential by taking on these roles, but it's unlikely to be in the long term interests of the organization. The best defence against this risk is to reflect on each review (perhaps by having someone on the review team act as an observer) and watch for signs of reviewers undertaking project management roles. If reviewers find that this is happening, they need to call it out as a problem.

REVIEWS AND MATURITY MODELS

Maturity models have become increasingly popular over recent years. They started with the CMM (Capability Maturity Model, Humphrey, 1989), which itself built from the work of people in the quality movement. The models are generally arranged into five levels, with a defined set of capabilities (typically organized by 'process areas') needed to progress from one level to the next. A number of project management and related models have appeared in recent years, for example P3M3 (Portfolio, Programme and Project Management Maturity Model, OGC, 2006) and OPM3 (Organizational Project Management Maturity Model, PMI, 2003).

These models can be a useful guide to organizational improvement efforts. They help answer questions such as 'What are we good at?', 'What are our weaknesses?' and 'Where should we focus next in our improvement efforts?'. At the same time, they can't substitute for careful thinking about an organization's capabilities, objectives and improvement strategy, just as a checklist can't substitute for a carefully conducted interview.

Where do reviews fit into an improvement effort based on such models? Looking at P3M3, it doesn't identify reviews as a process area in their own right. Instead, they are an aspect of most process areas. Thus the model assumes that an organization will have some capacity to conduct reviews before it engages in any deeper improvement efforts. P3M3 does give an indication of the type of reviews that an organization might conduct as it 'matures':

- Level 1: Senior management review projects and portfolios periodically. Projects are reviewed regularly to verify their continued alignment to the initial objectives and plans.

- Level 2: The organization also conducts formal reviews of programme briefs to assess their objectives and scope against the organization's capacity and capability to deliver, and to confirm that appropriate plans, controls, risk management, and so on, are in place. There is a clear brief for ongoing programme assurance, with formal tracking of the issues it raises. There is regular monitoring of the business case, and formal reviews at the end of tranches of work.

- Level 3: There is a defined policy for reviews, with trained review leaders and documented procedures. This policy covers areas such as review of benefits profiles and benefits realization strategies, quality assurance, monitoring of portfolio risk, and so on. Process development and improvement activities are also subjected to regular review.

- Level 4: Metrics to measure the effectiveness of project and programme reviews are recorded. Portfolio-level capacity reviews are introduced.

- Level 5: Reviews extend to cover problem management and ongoing process improvement activities.

The general trend is that, as maturity grows, then the organization reviews more rigorously (introduction of formally documented procedures and then of metrics) and more widely (looking at a wider range of artefacts and activities), but that a basic capacity to review must be there from the outset.

OPM3 does identify a number of specific review processes, for example covering portfolio and gate reviews. However, it also embeds reviews within the controls applied to most programme and portfolio management processes. So again, the ability to review is seen as a basic capability, necessary to any improvement effort.

CASE STUDY

Assuring Quality in a Global Application Portfolio

Logistics Company is a market leader in international express delivery, air freight, overland transport and shipping. From its base in Europe, it has major operations on all continents. Its IT infrastructure and application development portfolio mirrors these global operations.

WHAT IS THE SIZE AND SHAPE OF YOUR PROJECT PORTFOLIO?

We average about 6500 development days per year, refining and extending our internal, bespoke applications. These days are divided into a major release every three to four months, with about 1000 to 1200 days per release, plus some smaller projects and a 'bucket' of days for general application maintenance. We are also running a number of projects to integrate commercial-off-the-shelf products with our bespoke applications.

Most development is conducted by two offshore Indian vendors. Logistics Company retains responsibility for overall programme and project management, product management, software architecture, testing and service management.

WHAT SORT OF REVIEWS DO YOU PERFORM?

We conduct peer reviews of the business requirements prior to baselining. We then conduct weekly walkthroughs of key work products, such as high-level test plans, as they're developed. We also do retrospectives on all major programmes, and for the more problematic smaller projects.

HOW DO YOU CONDUCT THESE REVIEWS?

We use an approach based on the 'team of peers' model from Microsoft's Solution Framework. Review teams include people from roles such as Support, Product Management, Test Management and Project/Programme Management. On occasion, they also include Infrastructure specialists and even people from User Education. Each person is experienced in their particular role, and typically has a strong background in the business domain also.

Peer review teams are typically between six and 12 people. Walkthroughs are smaller – generally no more than six people. The amount of time they put into each review depends on the estimated size and complexity of the release, the quality of the initial business requirements, and so on. We use quality metrics to determine the business case for how much to invest in reviews.

WHAT VALUE DO THE REVIEWS ADD?

Assumptions used to be a big issue – we had a tendency to rush into 'solution mode'. People also had a poor understanding of quality attributes/non-functional requirements. Through a combination of reviews and training, we now have more predictable delivery, reduced field-error-rates and a reduced cost-of-poor-quality.

WHAT CHALLENGES DO REVIEW TEAMS RUN INTO?

Most projects include internal people from at least two regions out of Europe, America and Asia-Pacific, and our vendors have 70–80 per cent of their teams based offshore. So communication can be a big challenge. It helps that our internal teams now have several years of working together across different cultures, but we still need to manage breakdowns of communications periodically. It's been important for senior management to set a good example here, for example , explaining that to manage a programme like this, you need open, honest communication and clear visibility through performance metrics.

We also need to manage basic logistical things like the timing of reviews. Time zones are a constant challenge: we rotate reviews on a weekly basis so that one team doesn't constantly have to start work at 05:00 or finish at 22:00.

The limited availability of internal software architects is another challenge. We have four architects to carry out reviews covering 6,500 development days, and both suppliers have tended to overuse one subject matter expert in particular. By using sampling and time-boxed reviews, we've improved the understanding of all parties and hence some of the dependency on these key people.

WHAT CHALLENGES HAVE YOU RUN INTO IN SETTING UP THE REVIEW PROCESS?

People have taken time to accommodate new ways of working. Some members of internal teams with many years of domain experience tended to make assumptions about what can be 'reasonably expected' from a supplier. There can also be a lot of resistance to taking part in training. People say: 'I've been doing this job for 20 years. It's insulting to expect me to go on a course.' Again, senior management support and coaching has been important to address this.

Suppliers can also be resistant to change. Initially the two vendors were at very different levels of 'maturity' themselves. One was CMMi (Capability Maturity Model integrated) Level 5. The other had been SW-CMM (Software Capability Maturity Model) Level 5 but over time had dropped off the CMM model altogether. The latter vendor was very resistant to change and seemed to be convinced that these process improvements would increase effort rather than reduce it.

ACKNOWLEDGEMENTS

With thanks to Phil Stubbington.

Team Issues

Just as project teams and other stakeholders have to plan to accommodate the impact of reviews on their activities, review teams need to plan for a number of stress factors as they interact with the rest of the organization. It's easy for reviewers to become isolated, outside the mainstream career path and with little appreciation for the contribution they make to projects' success. After all, it's project managers and sponsors who generally, and rightly, receive credit for delivering a project.

In extremis, reviewers can find themselves in a highly stressful situation, in conflict with the project manager and sponsor about the status of a project and with little organizational support. I've seen reviewers who started to doubt their own sanity: they could see clear signs of major problems on a project, yet the project manager, sponsor and everyone else they spoke to dismissed their views. They started to wonder if they were seeing things. Without appropriate support, this stress can derail a review team.

This chapter discusses ways to build this support. It starts by describing some of the stress factors on reviewers. It then looks at some of the things we can do to mitigate these stresses. One of the key ways to do this is to build a team that projects professionalism and is confident of its skills. Thus, the chapter closes by looking briefly at some of the skills that reviewers need, and at options for building these skills.

STRESS FACTORS

In many ways, becoming part of a dedicated review team is an odd thing for a project manager or similar professional to do. Project managers tend to be hands-on people, priding themselves on their ability to make things happen. Project review and assurance teams, on the other hand, tend to play a supporting role. They observe, analyse and recommend. They influence a variety of stakeholders without ever really exerting any significant degree of control. They frame their communications very carefully, constantly aware of nuances of tone and meaning. It can feel like they are always politicking, never acting.

Some people get frustrated with this lack of direct control. Other factors that reviewers may need to deal with include:

- Constant shift of focus: Rather than managing a single project through to completion, each reviewer may be spread across a portfolio of projects. They may touch these projects only at a small number of points in their lifecycle, never seeing any of them to the end. Again, some people find this constant shift of attention frustrating. (Others, of course, prefer to work this way, and everyone can learn from seeing a wide range of approaches in a short period of time.)

- Constant need to prove your credentials: Each time a reviewer meets a new project team, they are being assessed. Why should we believe you? How are you going to know as much about our project after two days as we do after three months of working on it? In some environments, this can be very draining.

- Need to understand and accept different perspectives: Project teams may choose approaches that reviewers wouldn't have considered – unusual tools and technologies, for example, or controversial development styles. Reviewers need to put their own preferences on hold and focus on whether the project team, with its mix of skills and resources, can make the chosen approach work. Objectively assessing and monitoring an approach you wouldn't normally use can be hard. Being able to say 'That's not how I would have done it, but I think you can make it work' can be even harder.

- Managing relationships while maintaining objectivity: As reviewers spend time with a project, they build relationships with the team. At the same time, they need to maintain enough distance to be able to objectively assess the project team's assumptions, expectations, status reports, and so on. It can be easy to get the balance wrong, either 'going native' or adopting an overly adversarial relationship, or to oscillate between the two extremes.

- Dealing with conflict: As noted at the start of this chapter, reviewers sometimes find themselves in conflict with project teams and sponsors. They can also experience conflicting agendas within the review team – where reviewers represent different members of the project board, with different objectives, for example. It can be difficult to maintain objectivity and perspective while dealing with such conflict.

- Fear about loss of skills: If people have been seconded to a review team for a sustained period, they may become concerned that their primary skill as a project manager or other professional is becoming eroded through lack of hands-on usage. This can be particularly worrying for specialists in fast-moving technical areas.

- Being on the margin: Finally, reviewers are always on the margin of the projects they deal with. They're often not invited to project celebrations, for example. Likewise, they can be on the margin of the organization, outside mainstream career paths and seen as observers rather than direct contributors to success.

Just knowing what to expect can make it easier for reviewers to deal with these factors. Beyond that, review teams need to build support structures that will help them manage this stress. Of course, organizations also have an incentive to build such structures, not least because reviewers' performance will degrade if they don't cope with the stress.

(Many of these stresses apply primarily to dedicated reviewers. Peer reviewers who spend only a small proportion of their time reviewing are less likely to be exposed to many of them. Nonetheless, even if your community is composed primarily of part-time reviewers, it can be worth building some of the following support structures.)

REVIEW TEAM SUPPORT

What sort of support structures might review teams build for themselves? I'd consider providing support in five ways:

1.   creating an organizational home for reviewers;

2.   developing strong internal communications;

3.   rotation of roles;

4.   addressing organizational infrastructure;

5.   celebrating success.

ORGANIZATIONAL HOME

Reviewers don't just communicate project issues: like all employees, they want to be involved in communications about organizational strategy, operations and suchlike. Nothing adds to the sense of marginalization like not hearing about organizational initiatives because 'no-one thought to tell you guys'. So reviewers need a clear position within the organizational structure. Giving reviewers such a home helps them to maintain a distinct identity and gives them a clear route for communicating with senior management and other parts of the organization.

Chapter 9 discussed some of the trade-offs of positioning an assurance team within a corporate PMO. Provided that the challenges of maintaining independence are managed, this can be a reasonable home for reviewers. Likewise, if their role is primarily portfolio-level assurance, aligning them to the office of the Chief Operating Officer (COO) or CFO can make sense.

Wherever the reviewer's organizational home is placed, it can eliminate a lot of stress simply by providing basic logistical support. Having someone to coordinate schedules, arrange travel, manage expense claims, and so on, can make life easier for reviewers. Beyond this, a central office can help manage many aspects of the review process. For example, it might deal with:

- finding or developing training courses for reviewers, negotiating rates with training providers, and so on;

- gathering and assessing feedback from project teams about the effectiveness of reviews;

- managing databases of reviews undertaken, issues identified, action lists, and so on;

- summarizing reviewer's reports to develop case studies, examples of good practice, analysis of common issues on projects, and related assets.

All of this takes load off the reviewers, freeing them to focus on undertaking reviews and managing relationships with project teams and other stakeholders.

INTERNAL COMMUNICATIONS

By constructing a strong internal communication network, reviewers can support each other, share experiences and lessons learned, and test their observations and findings against a sympathetic audience. These all help to avoid isolation and to manage the other stress factors.

Where reviewers are grouped into stable teams, they will naturally provide much of this support for their team-mates. Even so, it can be worth building other communication mechanisms, both to extend the team's communication network and to manage risks such as groupthink. Where teams are restructured regularly, or where reviewers often operate individually, extended communication networks are invaluable. Consider communication structures such as:

- Regular conference calls to share news and concerns across the reviewer community: Short calls with a well-defined agenda tend to work best. If an issue needs more than a couple of minutes of discussion, it's worth setting up a follow-on session for those who are interested. I like to schedule conference calls at a defined weekly slot: if people miss one call, they know they'll be able to catch up the following week.

- Periodic face-to-face meetings to discuss broader issues, agree strategy and make personal contact: If reviewers are distributed or very mobile, it makes a big difference to the quality of their relationships and support network if they get together for a day periodically. Some organizations see such meetings as an overhead, but they generally improve communication within the community significantly.

- Pairing reviewers to mentor and support each other: Over time, pairs get to know each other's projects, personal strengths, and so on, so are able to provide deep support for each other. Being able to test ideas and share thoughts with someone who understands your context can make it easier to think through the situation on a project, and to report on it clearly and firmly. A good mentor will also challenge your thinking, ensuring your reasoning is well structured and doesn't overlook key facts.

- Encouraging project teams to include reviewers in their team events and celebrations.

And, of course, all the facilities of electronic communication – email, instant messaging, discussion boards, and so on – are available. If reviewers are mobile, it's worth ensuring they have the appropriate technology to connect easily to these services.

ROTATION OF ROLES

Reviewing is a great way for project professionals to extend their experience by seeing a wide range of projects. Many people will then want to capitalize on this experience by applying it to a project of their own. Rotating people through the review team can thus meet several goals. It provides a route for people to build experience and then take it back to their projects. It ensures that review teams are staffed with people who are actively engaged in delivering projects, which can help build credibility with project teams. And it means that people only need to deal with the stress factors for a defined period.

This raises the question of how long people should spend on a review team. Short secondments may mean that reviewers don't get time to fully develop reviewing skills, thus limiting their effectiveness. There is also a risk that people will see reviewing as a secondary activity, only performed in the 'dead time' between 'real' work on projects. Long secondments raise all the concerns about losing touch with projects and eroding skills. My rule of thumb is to second reviewers for about the length of a typical project in the organization. This gives reviewers the chance to see some projects through their entire lifecycle, which is a great way to learn.

If reviewers are staffed to relatively stable review teams, then it may also be useful to rotate people around these teams occasionally. This exposes people to different approaches and experience.

ORGANIZATIONAL INFRASTRUCTURE

Dealing with organizational details can drain a lot of energy and morale. When setting up the organizational home for reviewers, ensure that the necessary infrastructure is in place. This includes technical support for computers and communications equipment, clear processes for handling expenses and other administration, and so on.

Human resources processes can be an important aspect of this infrastructure. Is there a clear career path for reviewers? If reviewers are being seconded from other activities, will the experience they gain be appropriately recognized? Are pay and incentive plans set up appropriately?

CELEBRATING SUCCESS

Chapter 10 noted the need to gather success stories in order to demonstrate the value that reviews are adding and to support their ongoing business case. This information can also help reviewers to build self-belief and maintain morale.

So spread the message about the positive impact that reviews are having, share positive feedback from project teams and other stakeholders, and take the opportunity to celebrate notable successes.

DEVELOPING REVIEWER SKILLS

Many of the stress factors arise from the complex relationship between reviewers, project teams and other stakeholders. If reviewers are confident of their skills and able to project professionalism, they will be better placed to manage these relationships and hence avoid the stresses. This raises two questions: what skills should we be looking for in our reviewers, and how might we develop those skills?

Here are some of the skills and experience I'd be looking for in a reviewer:

- Experience of projects of similar or larger magnitude to the projects being reviewed: Reviewers with an established track record will be better placed to gain the respect of project teams, and to get up to speed with projects and likely issues.

- Experience of a range of different types of project: This breadth of experience helps people understand different approaches and trade-offs, and to identify the risks and issues associated with any given approach.

- Strong professional background: Reviewing is typically seen as a project management skill. I'd certainly want strong project management skills on most review teams, but other skills can also be valuable: business analysis, procurement, contract management, technical specialisms. I'd therefore be looking for each reviewer to have a strong professional background in either project management or one of these skills.

- Interpersonal skills: The ability to build trust and rapport with project team members is particularly important. Thus, I'd be looking for things such as listening skills, the ability to see both sides of an issue, and a strong sense of professionalism and integrity. Reviewers also need to be able to hold their ground and argue a case without becoming overly aggressive or defensive.

- Hard reviewing skills: Reviewers need to be able use the team's processes, checklists and tools. (These skills can all be developed through training.)

- Soft reviewing skills: Attention to detail and the patience to gather evidence can be very valuable, as is the ability to analyse this information and build a clear chain of reasoning. Curiosity and creativity also help reviewers to see the project from different perspectives and hence identify issues that others aren't seeing. Reviewers need courage to give bad news. And, of course, they need strong observation and interviewing skills.

Each review team may have one or two people who don't fully fit this profile, for example, junior people who are learning the ropes or technical specialists who are focused on one aspect of the project.

How do we build such skills? People need to bring the professional background and experience with them. Thus a training and development programme for reviewers will probably focus on the interpersonal and soft and hard reviewing skills. A balanced programme might cover:

- Hard reviewing skills: Many of these can be developed through standard training techniques (classroom or online), followed by practical experience on reviews.

- Soft reviewing and interpersonal skills: Some of these are innate, but they can be further developed through simulations and experiential training, and by techniques such as apprenticing people on review teams. Pairing reviewers to mentor each other and encourage reflection on their personal strengths and weaknesses can also help develop these skills.

Finally, it can be invaluable to gather feedback from project teams to help reviewers identify and reflect upon their strengths and weaknesses. It may be worthwhile to supplement this information with internal observation and monitoring (e.g. designating one person on a review team to observe the team's practices and identify opportunities for improvement). The case study *Review Techniques in the Education Sector* illustrates such an approach to developing review teams.

Completion Bonds in the Film Industry

The people financing films and television productions often seek independent assurance that the producer will deliver to the agreed timescale and budget. Under a Completion Guarantee, a specialized insurance company (the guarantor) provides this assurance. The guarantor takes a very active role to identify risks affecting the project and to help the producer mitigate them. If the producer fails to mitigate the risks, the guarantor may even step in to complete the production rather than face a claim from the financiers. Thorough review processes play an important part in the identification and management of the guarantor's risks.

Risk identification begins with the 'specification' for the production. Before giving a guarantee, the guarantor conducts a thorough review of the script, crew, production schedules, budgets, and so on. They meet with key members of the production team (e.g. the producer, production accountant, and director of photography) to confirm that appropriate direction and controls are in place, that the plans are feasible, and that the team has the necessary skills and experience to deliver them.

The guarantor then actively monitors status throughout the production. They will require progress reports showing what scenes have been shot, how many people have been on set, what materials have been used, and so on, perhaps even on a daily basis. They will review details of what's been spent against the budget. They retain the right to visit the set at any time, unannounced, and to meet with anyone involved with the production.

If the production runs into difficulties, the guarantor may take control of the troubling aspects. They may, for example, impose additional financial controls or seek changes to the script or personnel. In extremis, they may bring in their own producer to take control of the whole project. If the film still can't be delivered, then the guarantor repays the original financing. In the UK, the guarantor steps in at some level on about one in five films.

This can make for a complex relationship between the guarantor and the producer. The producer has first responsibility for delivering the project. They have an intimate knowledge of the film and how it will be realized. They are likely to live out the day-to-day details of setting up and managing the production. So the guarantor will want to maintain as open and productive a relationship as possible with the producer. At the same time, the guarantor has a contractual obligation to step in to ensure that the film is delivered if the producer runs into difficulties. They're not just a friendly mentor.

This sort of scrutiny is not unusual: it's the norm in the industry. Independent producers expect it as a condition of obtaining financing, so they learn to live with it. Ideally, the producer is able to use the guarantor as an additional resource, to help spot risks and think through ways to deal with them before they blow up.

For the financier, a completion guarantee helps bound their investment risk and provides access to independent expertise to actively manage production risks. A completion guarantee may cost between 2 per cent and 6 per cent of the total production budget, but that's a price many are prepared to pay for effective risk management.

ACKNOWLEDGEMENTS

With thanks to Laurent Bossavit for initial discussion of completion bonds.

Additional materials taken from:

- Skillset Film, 2007–08;

- Patrimoine canadien, 2005;

- Allen Financial Insurance Group, n.d.

Conclusion

Projects are risky activities. By definition, they are about doing new things, outside the bounds of an organization's routine activities. They may require us to assemble large teams of people with diverse backgrounds, perspectives and agendas. They generally operate under significant time and budgetary pressures. Factors such as new technologies add to the risks. It's scarcely surprising that some projects fail.

Projects begin to fail when they lose touch with reality. A range of symptoms may ultimately lead us to recognize the failure: missed milestones, unacceptable deliverables, blown budgets, burnt-out teams. However, most of these symptoms arise from some earlier failure to recognize that the project's actual performance was diverging from the planned path. Rather than correct this divergence, we stuck with the plan. We managed the plan rather than the reality.

Many of the techniques of project management are about keeping in touch with reality. We establish a clear plan to make it a little more obvious when we've gone off the path. We think through risks so that we can recognize them easily when they do occur. Our status reports and controls are all about building a clear picture of what's going on and dealing with any deviations. Unfortunately, the people who undertake all these activities are subject to a range of human biases that make it all too easy to avoid painful realities until it's too late to fix them.

For an organization, the secret to success is not to eliminate these failures. That would mean doing no projects. Organizations need to take risks in order to obtain the benefits that projects can deliver: new products, improved processes, better infrastructure, and so on. The secret to success, rather, is to learn from the failures. If an organization can identify failures (and potential failures) rapidly, correct them and move on, it can change and improve. In a successful organization, this learning will happen at three levels:

- Projects will learn from the outcomes of their initial activities, constantly reframing their approach to accommodate this new information.

- The organization will learn from its projects, building a 'memory' of what does and doesn't work and sharing that across its portfolio.

- People will learn from their experiences, enhancing their skills and competencies to deliver future projects.

Project reviews can aid all of these learning processes. They can help project teams keep in touch with the immediate reality of what is happening on their projects, and hence to learn from and deal with this reality. They can record their observations into checklists and other artefacts, and hence take the lessons learned on each project out into the wider organization. They can give people access to a wider range of skills and expertise, both through mentoring and through the experience of participating on review teams. Project reviews are a great way to help organizations keep in touch with reality, and to learn from it.

There are many ways to conduct a project review. When setting up a review programme, we need to consider factors such as the timing of reviews, their objectives, the level of independence of the review team, the degree of formality of the review process, the standards that we will review against, and so on. Successful reviewers will be able to consider all of these factors. Above all, they will be able to do three things:

- Set up and execute reviews effectively: Reviews are often performed to tight timescales and in the face of a variety of political pressures. A review team with a clear understanding of the processes it will follow and the assets (e.g. checklists and reference models) it can bring to bear will be able to hit the ground running and project professionalism. That makes it easier to deal with these pressures.

- Deliver actionable outputs: Reviewers need to understand their audience, the information it needs in order to make decisions and the actions it can take to improve the project. It is only by framing their findings in a way that this audience can hear them and act on them that the review team can add any real value.

- Set up appropriate support structures for themselves: Reviewing can be a stressful occupation. It is easy for reviewers to become isolated or marginalized. It is only by framing their findings in a way that this audience can hear and then act upon, that the review team can add any real value.

I firmly believe that project reviews can deliver significant value to most organizations. This is partly because their projects will be delivered more effectively. At least as importantly, the organization's managers and executives will have reliable information about their projects, enabling them to make better decisions and to have the confidence to take well-judged risks. In this way, they can help their organization to grow and evolve. I hope this book will help you to execute such reviews.

Bibliography

Allen Financial Insurance Group, n.d., *Film Production Completion Bond* (http://www.eqgroup.com/completion_bond.htm).

Association for Project Management (APM), 2006, *APM Body of Knowledge, 5th Edition.*

Beck, K. and Andres, C., 2004, *Extreme Programming Explained: Embrace Change.* Addison Wesley.

Brooks, F., 1995, *The Mythical Man Month, 2nd Edition.* Addison Wesley.

Chism, N.V.N., 2007, *Peer Review of Teaching: A Sourcebook.* Anker.

Derby, E. and Larsen, D., 2006, *Agile Retrospectives: Making Good Teams Great.* Pragmatic Bookshelf.

Dickens, C., 2004[1850], *David Copperfield.* Penguin Classics.

Dickens, C., 2003[1857], *Little Dorrit.* Penguin Classics.

Gilb, T. and Graham, D., 1993, *Software Inspection.* Addison Wesley.

Hammersley, M. and Atkinson, P., 1995, *Ethnography: Principles in Practice.* Routledge.

HM Treasury, 2007, *Transforming Government Procurement.* HMSO.

Humphrey, W., 1989, *Managing the Software Process.* Addison Wesley.

Institute on Governance (IOG), n.d., website (http://www.iog.ca).

ISACA, 2008, *COBIT 4.1 is Available!* (http://www.isaca.org/cobit).

Johnson, J., 2006, *My Life is Failure.* The Standish Group International Inc.

Kaner, S., Lind, L., Berger, D., Toldi, C. and Fisk, S., 1996, *The Facilitator's Guide to Participatory Decision Making.* New Society Publishers.

Kerth, N.L., 2001, *Project Retrospectives: A Handbook for Team Reviews.* Dorset House.

National Audit Office (NAO), 2006, *Central Government's Use of Consultants.* The Stationery Office.

Office of Government Commerce (OGC), 2002, *Management of Risk: Guidance for Practitioners.* The Stationery Office.

Office of Government Commerce (OGC), 2004a, *Managing Successful Programmes.* The Stationery Office.

Office of Government Commerce (OGC), 2004b, *OGC Gateway Process Review Pack.* The Stationery Office.

Office of Government Commerce (OGC), 2004c, *OGC Gateway Low Risk Workpack* (CD). The Stationery Office.

Office of Government Commerce (OGC), 2005, *Managing Successful Projects with PRINCE2*. The Stationery Office.

Office of Government Commerce (OGC), 2006, *Portfolio, Programme and Project Management Maturity Model (P3M3)*. The Stationery Office.

Office of Government Commerce (OGC), 2008, a large number of materials (e.g. checklists) are available from their website (http://www.ogc.gov.uk/) .

Office of Government Commerce (OGC), n.d., *ITIL: 'The Key to Managing IT Services'* (http://www.ogc.gov.uk/guidance_itil.asp).

OFSTED, 2005, *Framework for the Inspection of Schools in England from September, 2005*. HMSO.

OFSTED, 2006, *Conducting the Inspection: Guidance for Inspectors of Schools*. HMSO.

Patrimoine canadien, 2005, *Completion Guarantees and Other Insurance, and Financial Instruments Used by Canadian Producers* (http://www. patrimoinecanadien.gc.ca/progs/ac-ca/progs/rc-tr/market/publications/ etude_sur_les_garanties-bond_study/5_e.cfm).

Project Management Institute (PMI), 2003, *Organisational Project Management Maturity Model (OPM3)*. Project Management Institute, Inc.

Project Management Institute (PMI), 2004, *A Guide to the Project Management Body of Knowledge, Third Edition*. Project Management Institute, Inc.

Richards, K., 2007, *Agile Project Management: Running PRINCE2 Projects with DSDM ATERN* TSO. The Stationery Office.

Schwaber, K., 2003, *Agile Project Management with Scrum*. Microsoft Press.

Skillset Film, 2007–08, website (http://www.skillset.org/film/knowledge/ article_5105_1.asp).

Smith, C., 2007, *Making Sense of Project Realities*. Gower Publishing.

Standish Group, 1995, *The Standish Group Report, Chaos*. The Standish Group International, Inc.

Standish Group, 2006, *The Standish Group Report, Chaos*. The Standish Group International, Inc.

Thompson, C.B., 2002, *Interviewing Techniques for Managers*. McGraw-Hill.

Ullman, D.G., 2006, *Making Robust Decisions: Decision Making for Technical, Business and Service Teams*. Trafford.

Virine, L. and Trumper, M., 2007, *Project Decisions: The Art and Science*. Management Concepts.

Weigers, K.E., 2002, *Peer Reviews in Software*. Addison-Wesley.

Weinberg, G.M., 1994, *Quality Software Management: Vol. 3: Congruent Action*. Dorset House.

Wheatley, M., 2005, *The Importance of Project Management.* (http://www.projectsmart.co.uk/the-importance-of-project-management.html).

4ps, 2006, supports Gateway™ reviews, derived from OGC processes, for local government in UK: a large number of materials are available on their website (http://www.4ps.gov.uk).

Index

About the Author

Graham Oakes helps people untangle complex technology, relationships, processes and governance. As an independent consultant, he helps organizations such as Vodafone, Sony Computer Entertainment, The Open University, the Council of Europe and the Port of Dover to define strategy, initiate projects and hence run those projects effectively. Prior to going independent, he was Director of Technology at Sapient Limited, where he ran the project review process for the UK Business Unit. Before that he was Head of Project Management for Psygnosis Ltd (a subsidiary of Sony), where he ran Independent Project Assurance teams working across the UK, Europe and the USA.

Graham writes a regular column for EvaluationCentre.com (now part of the National Computer Centre), and occasional articles for publications such as the *Financial Times*, *Free Software Magazine* and *Project Magazine*. He was a medallist in the British Computer Society IT Consultancy of the Year Awards for 2007.

Graham can be contacted at graham@grahamoakes.co.uk or through his website, www.grahamoakes.co.uk.